The IMPERIAL IMPRESARIO

ALSO BY CHRISTOPHER JOLL

Uniquely British: A Year in the Life of the Household Cavalry

The Speedicut Papers, Books 1–9

The Speedicut Memoirs, Books 1–6

WITH ANTHONY WELDON
The Drum Horse in the Fountain

WITH CORIE MAPP
Black Ice: The Memoir of Corie Mapp

The IMPERIAL IMPRESARIO

The Treasures, Trophies & Trivia of Napoléon's Theatre of Power

CHRISTOPHER JOLL & PENNY COBHAM

Nine Elms Books

First published in 2021
by Nine Elms Publishing
Clapham North Arts Centre,
26–32 Voltaire Road, London SW4 6DH

E *info@nineelmsbooks.co.uk*
W *www.nineelmsbooks.co.uk*

Text © Christopher Joll & Penny Cobham 2021

ISBN 978-1-910533-62-8 HB

Cover and text design, typesetting and layout
by Lyn Davies *www.lyndaviesdesign.com*
Text set in Rory Snow's *Barbou*
Printed and bound in India
by Imprint Press.

CONTENTS

THIS BOOK IS DEDICATED
TO THE MEMORY OF
His Imperial & Royal Majesty

NAPOLÉON I

Emperor of the French
& King of Italy

FOREWORD

The Duke of Richmond and Gordon

In the autumn of 1814, several months before the Battle of Waterloo, my ancestor, the 4th Duke of Richmond, moved to Brussels 'on an economical plan', where the cost of living was much less expensive than Britain. He took his large family with him and they rented a house on the Rue de la Blanchisserie.

In the days leading up to the Battle of Waterloo in 1815, an endless round of balls and dinners kept everyone amused as the city filled with soldiers preparing to fight Napoléon. On the evening of 15th June, Charlotte, Duchess of Richmond hosted a ball at their home. The arrival of a messenger half-way through set in train a sequence of events that culminated in the Battle of Waterloo three days later, thus making the ball arguably the most famous in history.

The ball itself was held in a wing of the Richmonds' house that had formerly been used as a coach showroom. By an extraordinary historical coincidence, the opposite wing was the former workshop where Napoléon's campaign carriage had been constructed three years previously. It was this carriage, known as *La Dormeuse*, which was captured on the evening of the 18th June, near Genappe. Its contents provided The Prince Regent, the King of Prussia, and many other collectors since then, with a trove of Napoléonica, much of which is described in the pages that follow.

Following the Battle of Waterloo, the Duke of Wellington gave my ancestor Napoléon's campaign chair as a token of gratitude for hosting the ball and remaining calm at a pivotal moment. It remains one of the most precious items in the collection at Goodwood and is in daily use. Therefore, it gives me great pleasure to write the Foreword to this book, which provides a fascinating look at the by-products of the Napoléonic era – a remarkable period in European history

Charles Lennox, 4th Duke of Richmond

ACKNOWLEDGEMENTS

THE AUTHORS WOULD LIKE to thank His Grace the Duke of Richmond and Gordon for writing the Foreword; John Hudson, the noted collector and dealer in Napoléonica, whose comprehensive archive of auction catalogues and sale results was invaluable; Tim Knox, Director of the Royal Collection Trust, who first suggested this book and was enormously helpful with access to, and comments on, the Napoléonica in the Royal Collection; the late Viscount Norwich, whose tale of The Prince Regent's imperial silver potties led us to the Bullock Museum sale of 1819; Nick Varney of Merlin Entertainments for permission to access the Madame Tussaud archive; Angela Jobson and Julia Maynard of Madame Tussauds for help with sifting through their extraordinary archive; Emma Floyd and the Paul Mellon Centre for Studies in British Art, for access to their archive of auction catalogues; Jean-Christophe Chataignier of the French auction house, Osenat; Helen Dorey at Sir John Soane's Museum; Bonhams the auctioneers for their assistance with some of the background history; Philip Mould, the London art dealer, broadcaster and star of the TV series, *Fake or Fortune*, for his views on the value of the painting lost in the Madame Tussaud fire in 1925; Samantha Wyndham for her meticulous edit of the manuscript; Lyn Davies of Lyn Davies Design for his beautiful design of the book and its cover; Anthony Weldon of Nine Elms Books for having the faith to publish this book; and, finally, Her Majesty The Queen for her Gracious Permission to use images in this book from the Royal Collection Trust.

TIMELINE

THE RISE & FALL OF NAPOLÉON

'Ability is nothing without opportunity'

1769   54th year of the reign of Louis XV ✹ 15th August: Napoléone di Buonaparte is born at Casa Buonaparte, Ajaccio, Corsica, which had been ceded to France by Genoa shortly before his birth.

1774   Louis XVI ascends the French throne.

1779   January: Napoléone di Buonaparte is enrolled at a religious school in Autun, France ✹ May: Napoléone di Buonaparte transfers with a scholarship to the Military School at Brienne-le-Château.

1784   Napoléone di Buonaparte is admitted to the École Militaire, Paris.

1785   September: Napoléone di Buonaparte is commissioned as a Second Lieutenant in La Fère artillery regiment.

1789   Outbreak of the French Revolution; Napoléone di Buonaparte applies to return to Corsica.

Storming of the Bastille, 14th July 1789

1792   War of the First Coalition (1792–1797) fought against France by Britain, Netherlands, Holy Roman Empire, Prussia, Naples, Portugal, Sardinia and Spain ❋ Aged 23 and a Captain, Napoléone di Buonaparte is given command, as a local Lieutenant Colonel, of a Battalion of Corsican republican volunteers ❋ Louis XVI deposed and First Republic established.

1793   Louis XVI executed ❋ Maximilien Robespierre elected to Committee of Public Safety, which instituted the Reign of Terror (*c.* 1793-94) ❋ Napoléone di Buonaparte changes his name to the French-sounding Napoléon Bonaparte and allies himself with Augustin Robespierre, younger brother of Maximilien ❋ Napoléon is appointed commander of the artillery at the Siege of Toulon (29th August – 19th December), wounded and promoted to Brigadier General, aged 24.

1794   Brigadier General Bonaparte devises a plan for the capture of the Kingdom of Sardinia ❋ *Coup d'État* of 9th Thermidor and the fall of Robespierre (27th July). Brigadier General Bonaparte is put under house arrest for two weeks.

1795   Brigadier General Bonaparte becomes engaged to Désirée Clary, sister of his brother Joseph's wife; in September he is removed from the list of Generals, for refusing an infantry command (effectively a demotion) with the Army of the West ❋ 13th Vendémiaire (5th October): this marks the turning point in Bonaparte's career, when he is appointed by Paul Barras to defend (successfully, with a 'whiff of grapeshot') the Convention, sitting in the Tuileries Palace, from a royalist insurrection ❋ Establishment of

Execution of Louis XVI,
21st January 1793

the Directory by Barras. Napoléon Bonaparte promoted by a grateful Barras to General and given command of the Army of Italy. Meets Vicomtesse Joséphine de Beauharnais, a former mistress of Barras.

1796 9th March: General Bonaparte marries Joséphine; takes command of the Army of Italy two days later  First Italian Campaign, fast-moving campaign including Battles of Castiglione, Bassano, Arcole and Rivoli.

Battle of the Pyramids, 21st July 1798

1797 By January, 1797, General Bonaparte has defeated the armies of Piedmont and Austria and has secured French control of northern Italy. He then moves to invade southern Austria and, by March, the Austrians sue for peace, ceding control of northern Italy, the Austrian provinces in the Low Countries, and giving France a free hand with the Republic of Venice, which General Bonaparte seizes on 12th May and comprehensively loots ❉ Coup of 18th Fructidor (4th September): General Bonaparte supports with troops Barras' coup against the royalists. General Bonaparte returns to Paris in December, meets Talleyrand (Foreign Minister) and starts to plan the invasion of Britain.

1798 Because of the strength of the Royal Navy, General Bonaparte abandons plans for the invasion and switches his attention to Egypt. The plan, agreed by the Directory, is to seize the Ottoman province, use it as a staging post to India, seize the lucrative British trade route with the East, forge an alliance with Tipu Sultan of Mysore, and so end British rule in India. General Bonaparte seizes Malta in June en route to Egypt, where he defeats the ruling Mamelukes in July at the Battle of the Pyramids. In August, the British fleet under Nelson destroys the French fleet at the Battle of Aboukir Bay ❉ War of the Second Coalition (Britain, Austria, Russia, Ottoman Empire, Portugal, Naples, Sweden and the German states, excluding Prussia) starts at the end of November.

Brumaire *coup d'État*, 9th November 1799

1799 General Bonaparte leads his Army against the Ottoman province of Damascus. After initial successes, he fails to take the fortress at Acre and withdraws his plague-stricken Army to Egypt where, on 25th July, he defeats an Ottoman counter-invasion. In August, with political affairs in Paris once more in flux, he returns without the Directory's permission to France, leaving his Army behind ❉ 18th Brumaire (9th November): General Bonaparte leads a *coup d'État* that topples the Directory and replaces it with a three-man Consulate, with himself as First Consul for a period of ten years, taking the Tuileries Palace as his residence. France is still *de jure* a republic but has become a *de facto* dictatorship.

1800 In the spring, First Consul Bonaparte leads the Army of Italy over the Alps to re-establish control of northern Italy, lost while he was in Egypt ❉

Execution of Duc d'Enghein,
21st March 1804

14th June: the Austrians are defeated at the Battle of Marengo but refuse to cede the territories; in December they suffer a second defeat at the Battle of Hohenlinden ※ Back in France, First Consul Bonaparte crushes successive Jacobin and royalist assassination plots.

1801   Treaty of Lunéville with Austria signed in February, confirming French territorial gains in Italy.

1802   27th March: the British sign the Treaty of Amiens bringing the War of the Second Coalition to an end ※ A plebiscite confirms First Consul Bonaparte as Consul-for-Life.

1803   Following the loss of its West Indian colonies, France sells the Louisiana Territories to the USA ※ War of the Third Coalition (Britain, Holy Roman Empire, Russia, Naples, Sicily and Sweden). In May, Britain blockades French ports. First Consul Bonaparte assembles an invasion force at Boulogne, which becomes the Grande Armée;

1804   January: Bourbon assassination plot uncovered, leading to abduction and execution of the Duc d'Enghien ※ 21st March: First Consul Bonaparte's Civil Code comes into force. To consolidate his position, Napoléon uses the assassination plot to create an imperial, dynastic system based on the Roman model; this is confirmed in a plebiscite ※ 18th May: Napoléon declared Emperor of the French. To consolidate loyalty of Army, he appoints eighteen Marshals of the Empire ※ 2nd December: Napoléon's Coronation is held at Notre Dame Cathedral in Paris.

1805   26th May: Napoléon is crowned as King of Italy in Milan Cathedral ※ Britain signs alliance with Russia; in August, faced with a threat from the east, Napoléon abandons his British invasion plan and marches the Grande Armée at great speed into the German states, crossing the Rhine in September ※ 16th – 19th October: Austrian forces are surrounded and defeated at Ulm ※ 21st October: the combined French and Spanish fleets are destroyed by a British fleet at the Battle of Trafalgar ※ In November, Vienna is occupied by the French Army ※ 2nd December: the combined armies of Russia and Austria are defeated at the Battle of Austerlitz ※ The year ends with the Treaty of Pressburg, removing Austria from the Allied coalition, and the creation of the French-controlled Confederation of the Rhine, which challenges Prussian supremacy over the minor German states.

1806   War of the Fourth Coalition (Prussia, Russia, Saxony, Sweden and Britain). Prussia commences hostilities in September; Prussian forces defeated in October at the Battles of Jena and Auerstedt. Napoléon's Berlin Decree establishes the Continental System, designed to isolate Britain by banning European trade with it.

1807   Russia joins forces with Prussia and clashes with Napoléon in February   Battle of Austerlitz,
        at the inconclusive Battle of Eylau ✺ 14th June: Napoléon achieves a   2nd December 1805
        crushing victory over the Russians at the Battle of Friedland, leading to
        the Treaty of Tilsit; in October, French troops under Murat enter Spain
        bound for Portugal which, as an ally of Britain, is breaching the
        Continental System.

1808   In the summer, Napoléon leads the Grande Armée into Spain, topples the
        legitimate Spanish King and replaces him with his brother, Joseph.

1809   In January, the British are driven out of Portugal at the Battle of Corunna
        ✺ War of the Fifth Coalition (Austria, Britain, Portugal and Spain) ✺
        10th April: Austrian forces invade France's ally, Bavaria; the Austrians are
        defeated in May at Battle of Eckmühl and Vienna is occupied for the
        second time; Napoléon then fails to cross the Danube at the Battle of
        Aspern-Essling in May, but succeeds in late June and inflicts a massive
        defeat on the Austrians at the Battle of Wagram, following which the
        Treaty of Schönbrunn is signed in October ✺ 14th December:
        Napoléon divorces Joséphine.

1810   1st April marries Erzherzogin (Archduchess) Marie Louise of Austria.

1811   20th March: birth of Napoléon's heir, the King of Rome.

1812   24th June: Napoléon invades Russia at the head of 450,000 men; 7th Sept-
        ember: the inconclusive Battle of Borodino is fought before Moscow, which
        the Russians then abandon and, subsequently, set on fire. Napoléon is

Battle of Borodino,
17th September 1812

forced to withdraw at the height of the winter (The Great Retreat); at Vilnius, on 5th December, Napoléon abandons the remnants of the Grande Armée and returns at speed to France.

1813 War of the Sixth Coalition (Austria, Prussia, Russia, Britain, Spain, Portugal and the minor German states) starts in March. Napoléon wins the Battle of Dresden in late August but, against overwhelming odd, loses the Battle of Leipzig on 19th October. French forces ousted from Spain by the British in November.

1814 In March, Paris is surrounded by the forces of the Sixth Coalition and capitulates. Napoléon hears of this at Fontainebleau and orders the Army to march on the capital but the Marshals refuse ✷ 4th April: under the Treaty of Fontainebleau, Napoléon abdicates in favour of his son and is exiled to Elba ✷ 6th April: restoration of the French monarchy with Louis XVIII ✷ 29th May: ex-Empress Joséphine, Duchesse de Navarre, dies at Malmaison; the allied powers convene in July for the Congress of Vienna.

1815 28th February: Napoléon lands with 700 men at Golfe Juin ✷ 20th March: Napoléon is in Paris at the head of a growing Army; Louis XVIII flees to Belgium ✷ 13th March: at the Congress of Vienna, the allies declare Napoléon an outlaw and launch the War of the Seventh Coalition (Austria, the minor German states, Denmark, Netherlands, Portugal, Prussia, Russia, Sicily, Spain, Sweden, Switzerland and Britain) ✷ By the start of June, Napoléon has forged c.300,000 men into the Army of the North, which he leads against a Prussian Army under Marshal Blücher and an

Battle of Waterloo, 18th June 1815

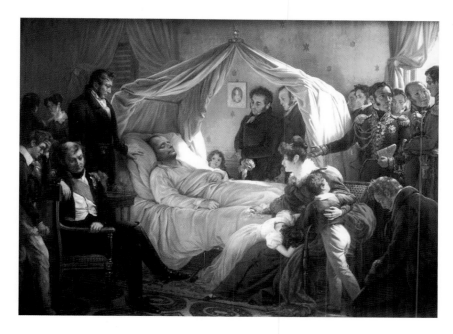

Death of Napoléon, 5th May 1821

allied Army led by the Duke of Wellington ✳ 16th June: at the Battle of Ligny the French Army forces the Prussians to withdraw, but without losing touch with Wellington ✳ 18th June: Napoléon attacks Wellington's defensive position at Waterloo but before he can take the position, late in the day the Prussians arrive and the battle is lost. Napoléon returns to Paris via Genappe, where he abandons his coach ✳ 22nd June: Napoléon abdicates for a second time and moves to Malmaison then to Rochefort, where he plans to go the USA, but the port is blockaded ✳ 15th July: Napoléon surrenders to the British and is exiled to St Helena.

1821　5th May: Napoléon dies (probably of stomach cancer) and, against his wishes, is buried in the Valley of the Willows on St Helena. Before his burial, a death mask is made and his penis is removed.

1840　Napoléon's well-preserved corpse is disinterred and returned to France, where he is given a State Funeral on 15th December.

1861　Napoléon's remains are transferred to a massive porphyry sarcophagus placed in a specially constructed open crypt under the dome of Les Invalides.

Napoléon's tomb at Les Invalides

AUTHORS' NOTE

William Bullock (*c.*1773–1849)

Marie Tussaud (1761–1850)

IN THE COURSE OF THIS narrative, frequent reference will be made to three highly important events in the history of Napoléonica. The first was the sale of a collection of items seized in the immediate aftermath of the Battle of Waterloo in 1815 and displayed at Bullock's Museum in the Egyptian Hall on London's Piccadilly, from where they were auctioned on Friday 11th June 1819. William Bullock is best described as an entrepreneur. His fortune was derived from his goldsmith and jewellery business in Birmingham, but his fame derives from his short-lived museum, variously known as Bullock's Museum, Bullock's Museum of Natural Curiosities, and the London Museum. The auctioneer at the 1819 sale of the museum's contents was Mr Bullock himself and the sale catalogue, annotated in his own hand with information on provenance, the prices paid and the names of the buyers, still exists and is extensively quoted here. So successful was the sale that Bullock commenced a third career as an auctioneer, using his vacant Piccadilly premises for the purpose.

Many of the items bought in the Bullock sale, and other items of Napoléonica that were acquired from Bullock before the sale or elsewhere, eventually ended up in Madame Tussaud's Exhibition on Baker Street. Sadly, they were all lost in the fire that devastated the upper floors of the building on the night of 18th March 1925. Known today for the waxworks that still bear her name, until the fire Marie Tussaud's exhibition was, in fact, more in the nature of a museum of curiosities of which the most important component was her collection of Napoléonica. Madame Tussaud, who was a French wax modeller, had experienced the excesses of the French Revolution at first hand, and moved to London in 1802. At first, she toured her exhibits around the United Kingdom until establishing her exhibition on a permanent site in London in 1836. When she died in 1850, Madame Tussaud's business was continued by three generations of her family, and it was her son and grandson who added much of the Napoléonica to the collection. In the course of the research for this book, the authors were given access to Madame Tussaud's Napoléonica archive, which includes a comprehensive catalogue of the items lost in the fire, prices paid for certain items and some images that are published here for the first time.

One of the Napoléonic tableaux
at Madame Tussaud's pre-1925

Lastly, on 15th and 16th November 2014, the bulk of the important collection of Napoléonica accumulated in the period 1922-1949 by Prince Louis II of Monaco was auctioned at Versailles by Osenat. Prince Louis was a former soldier and related to Napoléon through his mother, the grand-daughter of Stéphanie de Beauharnais, Grande Duchesse de Baden, who was the Emperor's adopted daughter and Joséphine's second cousin. His extensive collection of Napoléonica was exhibited in the Musée des Souvenirs Napoléoniens in the Palace of Monaco until the sale in 2014. The well-researched, two-volume catalogue for that sale has informed some of the contents of this book.

Prince Louis II of Monaco
(1870–1949)

NOTES

Titles and spelling   This is a very tricky subject on which there are no universal rules, the etiquette being different in each country. Accordingly, the co-authors have decided that in the interests of consistency, the titles and spelling of the names of the people included in this book are, for the most part, in their native language and as in use at the time they are mentioned. However, for ease of comprehension, their appointments and military ranks are expressed in English. The principal exceptions to this rule are the use of 'King' and 'Queen' rather than 'Roi' and 'Reine', and the English version of the titles of Napoléon and Joséphine. The practice on the continent of using the Christian name after the title is adopted here for non-British aristocrats. The names of non-British regiments are those which would have been used in English at that time, thus the '1er Régiment de Grenadiers-à-Pied de la Garde Impériale' is written as '1st Regiment of Grenadiers à Pied of the Imperial Guard'.

Dates   With certain exceptions, which are explained, the dates used throughout are those of the Gregorian calendar rather than the Julian calendar, then in use in Russia, or the French Republic calendar, which was in use in France from 1793 to 1805 and then again for nineteen days during the Paris Commune of 1871.

Napoléonic quotes   All the quotes in the chapter headings are attributed to Napoléon, but the attributions or the quotes may be apocryphal or shared with others.

Currency valuations   In 1800, one French Franc was worth £2.77 today. The difference between the value of the Pound at the time quoted and in 2020 has been computed using the Bank of England's inflation calculator.

Typography   Finally, as this book has been set in a late-eighteenth-century font, and the text has been ornamented with devices of the same period, the authors decided (with the enthusiastic support of their publisher) not to adopt the modern practice of using lower case for the first letter of titles, appointments and military formations.

INTRODUCTION

'In politics, stupidity is not a handicap"

IT IS NO COINCIDENCE that the membership of London's Garrick Club, whose motto is 'All The World's A Stage', has a higher proportion of politicians than actors amongst its members. Indeed, in the 1980s during Mrs Thatcher's administration, the Members' Bar at lunchtime frequently looked like an informal gathering of the Cabinet; but then politicians are, by default, actors. This is because, since time immemorial, politics has involved a great deal of 'performance' on the part of its practitioners: from the hustings to the debating chamber. A handful of actors, most notably the late President Ronald Reagan in the USA and Glenda Jackson CBE in the UK, have even abandoned the greasepaint in favour of the ballot box.

Tutankhamun's gold death mask

Enduring political stars are, however, rare and it is not just the script and the performances that generate longevity in office. In politics, as with the theatre, the supporting actors, the costumes, sets, props, merchandising, tours, reviews and the fan clubs are all part of the success or otherwise of the show, albeit – when it comes to make-up – varying in quality from the sublimity of Tutankhamun's gold death-mask to the bizarre haircut of President Kim Jong Un of North Korea.

Political power is also hedged around with a great deal of pageantry, which is nothing if it is not 'theatre', and which requires skilled choreography to make it work. That said, success at the time does not guarantee a legacy. The panoply of Persia's shahs and the rigid etiquette of Versailles under the Bourbons have vanished; the sinister sets made for Italy's Fascist and Germany's National Socialist rallies have all been swept away or repurposed; and Lord Mandelson's New Labour is no longer the roseate dream that it once was.

The same is true of political monuments. Despite carefully choreographed

A Nazi rally

ceremonies, monumentalised images in bronze and stone, and thornless red roses, the scenes of dictatorial triumphs, the grotesque statues and the scented imagery are all gone with the wind. Indeed, for the impresarios of power in Tripoli, Baghdad, Persepolis, Berlin, Rome and elsewhere, all that remains are fragments in paint, stone, brick, bronze, porcelain, silver and gold. As Percy Bysshe Shelley so eloquently expressed it in his poem Ozymandias, written in 1817:

I met a traveller from an antique land,
Who said "Two vast and trunkless legs of stone
Stand in the desert... Near them, on the sand,
Half sunk a shattered visage lies, whose frown,
And wrinkled lip, and sneer of cold command,
Tell that its sculptor well those passions read
Which yet survive, stamped on these lifeless things,
The hand that mocked them, and the heart that fed;
And on the pedestal, these words appear:
My name is Ozymandias, King of Kings;
Look on my Works, ye Mighty, and despair!
Nothing beside remains. Round the decay
Of that colossal Wreck, boundless and bare
The lone and level sands stretch far away."

This was not, however, the fate of perhaps the greatest of all political impresarios: Napoléon Bonaparte. For not only does most of his legacy remain, but unlike the Caesars, kings, dictators and spin doctors, who often had decades in power, it took Napoléon just a few years to create – in every conceivable medium – the enduring image of First Empire France as the nineteenth-century's version of Imperial Rome: an absolutist empire based on a revolutionary republic. From the larger-than-life marble statues to monogrammed silk stockings, the many tangible remains of this grand, imperial *mise en scène* have contrived to excite collectors, while his buildings and monuments still draw visitors in their hundreds of thousands.

Even more extraordinarily, the collecting of Napoléonica started while the man himself was still alive, and was led by his principal enemy, the portly Prince Regent (the future King George IV). While somewhat dementedly claiming the credit for toppling Napoléon, His Royal Highness stated openly his wish to exceed the Empire style, and was a serious collector of both French furniture of the period and personal items belonging to, or associated with, the Emperor. These intimate artefacts included Napoléon's Mameluke dressing gown and a brace of imperial gilt-lined silver chamber pots.

Percy Bysshe Shelley (1792–1822) by Alfred Clint

The Prince Regent, later King George IV (1762–1830)

The Prince Regent, or 'Prinny' as he was known at the time, was not, however, the only royal collector of Napoléonica. King Frederick William III of Prussia was delighted to receive the Emperor's hat, sword, and personal Orders and decorations, sent to him by Marshal Blücher (known to his troops as 'Marshal Forward') after Waterloo, which he put on a display at the Prussian Hall of Fame in the Zeughaus (Arsenal) Museum in Berlin. Now the German Historical Museum, all but the bicorne were 'acquired' by the Russians in 1945 and are held in the State Hermitage Collection. Queen Alexandra, as Princess of Wales, created a room at Marlborough House dedicated to Napoléon and filled it with French imperial memorabilia. Her daughter-in-law, the formidably acquisitive Queen Mary, bought or was 'given' a number of Bonaparte-related items, some of which were of dubious provenance; and Prince Louis II of Monaco created an entire Napoléonica museum in his tiny Mediterranean principality.

Beyond the courts of Europe, the collecting of items that had belonged to, or were associated with, the Emperor was shared by many leading figures of his day including the 6th Duke of Devonshire, the 3rd Earl of Onslow, and William Bullock, owner of Bullock's Museum on Piccadilly. Later collectors included Madame Tussaud and the 1st Viscount Leverhulme.

Today, in addition to the many extant buildings, monuments and works-of-art, contemporary souvenirs and personal items of Napoléonica can be found in numerous royal, national, military and private collections around the world, including those of the co-authors. When personal items of Napoléonica appear on the open market they command enormous prices. In 2014, when Prince Louis II's collection was sold to raise funds for the restoration of the palace in Monaco, one of the twenty or so surviving French-made bicorne hats worn by the Emperor sold for nearly €1.9 million (£1.5 million). Another example, with an impeccable provenance, sold at Sotheby's on 22nd September 2021 for €1,222,500 (£962,298) including the buyer's premium, which was more than four-times the estimate. Were it ever to come on the market, Napoléon's own diamond-encrusted snuff box, which sold in 1819 for £166 (2020: £14,880), would now sell for substantially more than his hat.

This is not, however, a book about Napoléon; that section of the library shelf is already overcrowded. Nor is it a comprehensive catalogue of museums with collections of Napoléonica; many such institutions, including the Musée Masséna in Nice and the Musée Marmottan in Paris are, with regret, not covered. It is, instead, a contextual examination of a representative cross-section of the relics from the Emperor's deliberately Roman-themed amphitheatre of power. Created under the aegis of the Imperial Impresario himself, these relics still exist in profusion – some with enormous value – two hundred years after his death in 1821 on St Helena.

CHAPTER ONE

CREATING THE STAR ROLE

'If you want a thing done well, do it yourself'

T IS A SIMPLE TRUTH of history that France only prospers under the firm hand of a charismatic leader wielding a high level of centralised power. However, since the French Revolution of 1789, the people of France have insisted that such quasi-dictatorial authority be tempered with at least the appearance of democracy. To address this dilemma, Napoléon Bonaparte, who had seized power in the *coup d'État* of 18th Brumaire (9th November) 1799, looked to history to cloak his regime in a shroud of republican legitimacy. The historical example he chose, for both the Consulate and the First Empire, was provided by Imperial Rome.

In brief, in 509 BC, the people of Rome, led by Lucius Junius Brutus and Lucius Tarquinius Collatinus, overthrew King Lucius Tarquinius Superbus, and established a diarchic republic. Its governing principle was embodied in the enduring tagline: *Senatus Populus Que Romanus* (The Senate and People of Rome), still to be found on modern manhole covers and elsewhere in the Eternal City. Brutus and Collatinus were the first two Consuls of this new republic, elected for a term of one year and sharing the powers of the former king. This they did in collaboration with the existing and unelected Senate, which traditionally dated its creation to 753 BC. With many changes, including the increasingly frequent appointment by the Senate of short-term dictators to hold the whole political fabric together, this system of Roman government survived until 27 BC. After a period of political and military chaos, the Senate then had no choice but to formalise the principle of dictatorial government by making Gaius Octavius, later known as Augustus Caesar, *Princeps Civitatis* (First Citizen) with pro-consular *imperium* (authority or power). The Roman Empire survived until 476 AD. Importantly for the principle of SPQR and for

Gaius Octavius, 63 BC – 14 AD

Napoléon, it remained (in theory at least) until its end a *de jure* republic, while operating *de facto* as an absolute monarchy or dictatorship.

Although not a carbon copy of Rome in 509 BC, the situation in France in 1799 was sufficiently analogous to give the new Consulate historical legitimacy when it was established by the leaders of the Brumaire Coup and later, in 1804, when it was replaced with the First Empire. However, as the mastermind behind both of these changes to the constitution of republican France, Napoléon knew that he needed more than an historical precedent to cement his power: the new system of French government had not only to be based on Roman principles, but must also be seen to look like the Roman republic and not a return to a French monarchy.

From this conviction arose the Empire style, and at its centre stood Napoléon Bonaparte, instantly recognisable – even in silhouette – wearing his bicorne hat and grey greatcoat, with a simple uniform beneath, and mounted on a pale grey Arab charger. However, as with all enduring roles, Napoléon's iconic image did not appear fully-formed at the start, but evolved as he climbed the greasy pole of power.

In the early days of his rise to supreme power, Napoléon, who had been born in Corsica on 15th August 1769, christened Napoléone di Buonaparte, and was the fourth child of Carlo and Maria-Letizia di Buonaparte (minor Tuscan and Genoese nobility respectively), had little money to expend on his image. This does not mean that he was unconscious of it: quite the contrary. In fact, he deliberately played down his origins as an aristocrat and a graduate of the royal

Napoléon on *Marengo* at Wagram, 5th-6th July 1809

École Militaire, by creating in their place the idealised image of a *sans-culottes* soldier of the Revolution. In a badly fitting uniform, with un-tied hair and revolutionary views, he established his credentials with the leaders of the Revolution including Robespierre and his murderous associates. Few if any contemporaneous images exist of Napoléon in this first role; such as do exist were created some years after the events depicted. However, by the Italian Campaign of 1796–7, artists were homing in on the image of the clean-shaven but wild-haired little General who gallantly captured the bridge of Arcole.

Napoléon Bonaparte on the Bridge of Arcole, 15th–17th November 1796

Significantly, at this point there were no signs, even in the pictures painted long after the event, of the Roman style that was to define the Consulate and the First Empire. The same is true of depictions of the Egyptian Campaign of 1798, in which the very un-Roman length of Napoléon's hair is a constant, and his portrayal astride a camel is a recurring theme. The French Revolution may have morphed into the Directory, but Napoléon had not yet changed his public profile.

Although the lack of a *coupe de cheveux* and the presence of the camels did not survive, two significant elements of the later imperial iconography did however emerge from the land of the Pharaohs. These were Egyptian motifs (including the sphynx, obelisk and palmette) and a six-year-old, 14.1 hands, pale grey Arab stallion, ever since identified as *Marengo*.

It is generally believed that Napoléon acquired this horse from the El Naseri Stud in 1798, although some sources state that the animal was the gift of Sheikh

Napoléon in Egypt, *c.* 1798

Napoléon's camel

Churchill in India, 1897

Napoléon on *Marengo* at
the Battle of the Pyramids,
21st July 1798

Khalil el Bakri, a member of the Great Diwan in Cairo. In whichever way the horse was acquired, on Napoléon's return to France the following year he brought the grey with him, along with two exotic-looking Mameluke servants (Roustam and Ali), further gifts from the Sheikh.

What he almost certainly did *not* ship back to France was the camel that, since 1933, has been on display at the Musée Africaine de l'île d'Aix. This is a museum founded by Baron Napoléon Gourgaud, a big game hunter and the great-grandson of General Gaspard Gourgaud, one of Napoléon's staff on St Helena. It is generally accepted that the Baron fabricated the origins of the camel to promote the museum to tourists.

Returning to *Marengo*, it was no accident that Napoléon chose such a showy mount for himself. Despite the horse's relatively small size, it stood out amongst its peers and thereby did the same for its rider. Exactly one hundred years later, a young British cavalry officer, similarly in search of early fame, had no hesitation in acquiring a pale-grey charger when he joined the Malakand Field Force, formed in 1897 to supress an uprising on the North-West Frontier of India. Writing to his mother, Lady Randolph Churchill, the young Winston Churchill explained the perils of making himself distinctive and an obvious target for Mohmand tribesmen:

'I must give you some account of my personal experiences on the 16th [September, 1897]. I started with the Cavalry and saw the first shot fired. After half-an-hour's skirmishing, I rode forward with the 35th Sikhs until firing got so hot that my grey pony was unsafe ... To ride a grey pony along a skirmish line is not a common experience; but I had to play for high stakes and have been lucky to win.'

Whether or not Churchill was deliberately copying Napoléon in his choice of mount, he almost certainly knew that, from 1798 onwards, the future Emperor was usually (but not invariably) depicted on a pale-grey Arab, whether crossing the Alps in 1800 or at subsequent battles from Spain in the west to Russia in the east and, most famously, at Waterloo. Nonetheless, while the image was (reasonably) constant, there must be some doubt as to whether or not it was the same horse.

For a start, the Battle of Marengo of 1800, after which the horse was allegedly named, was not fought until two years *after* Napoléon had acquired the Arab. Putting that to one side, it is also worth noting that, at the height of his power, Napoléon had more than fifty horses for his personal use in the Imperial Mews, including several greys with names that included *Sheikh*, *Distinguished* and *Sara*. Given that the primary purpose of the horse was to make its rider instantly recognisable, its name becomes of secondary importance.

Napoléon Crossing the Alps, May 1800

There must, therefore, be considerable uncertainty that the horse acquired by Napoléon in 1798 was the same one that lay wounded in a ditch at Waterloo in 1815. This injured horse, which nevertheless has ever since been identified as *Marengo*, was found by Lieutenant William Petre, 11th Baron Petre, of the 6th (Inniskilling) Dragoons. Having recognised the imperial shabraque and the brand-mark on the Arab's hind quarter, Petre saved the horse from the battlefield scavengers and nursed him back to health.

When Lord Petre returned to England later in 1815 he brought *Marengo* with him, and put the horse, with its imperial accoutrements, on public display at the Waterloo Rooms, 94 Pall Mall, London. Such was the horse's fame that thousands of people flocked to see him. Admission, and the opportunity to pet *Marengo*, who was advertised as 'so gentle that the most-timid Lady may approach him without fear', was one shilling (2020: £5) for adults and sixpence (2020: £2.50) for children and servants.

In 1824, having passed the horse around between various relations, Lord Petre sold *Marengo* to Captain John Julius William Angerstein of the 1st or Grenadier Guards. Angerstein was a grandson of the Russian-born John Julius Angerstein, who was Chairman of Lloyds of London, a founder of the Lloyd's Patriotic Fund for wounded servicemen and the dependants of those killed in action, and chairman of the public collection made for veterans of Waterloo and their families.

Angerstein junior put *Marengo* to stud at his property, New Barns near Ely, with a stud fee of £50 (2020: £5,613). Although the stallion sired two colts and a filly, none of them performed well on the turf. This disappointment notwithstanding, *Marengo* was allowed to see out his days in clover at Angerstein's country seat, Weeting Hall in Norfolk, dying in 1831 at the advanced age – if he was, indeed, the original horse – of thirty-eight, outliving his imperial master by ten years.

Following his demise, *Marengo*'s remains (less his two front hooves) were sent to the London Hospital, where his skeleton was articulated and then displayed at the Royal United Services Institution; it is now in the National Army Museum, London. Some ten years later Angerstein, by now a Guards Colonel, had the two front hooves shod with silver and converted, appropriately given the Emperor's addiction to the tobacco product, into snuff mills or boxes, albeit by different silversmiths and at different dates.

One snuff box, with silver mounts by Mortimer and Hunt and hallmarked 1841, was retained by the Angerstein family at Weeting Hall, complete with a lock of *Marengo*'s mane. In 1897, with the Angerstein fortune in steep decline thanks to race horses and the card table, their heavily-mortgaged house was repossessed by Norwich Union and the hoof disappeared. It was rediscovered in 1999 by an Angerstein descendant, wrapped in an old plastic bag in a kitchen drawer far from Norfolk. This hoof is currently on loan from the family to the Household Cavalry Museum at Horse Guards in London. Of the two snuff box hooves, it is the plainer, bearing only the single legend 'MARENGO' on the lid and naturalistic engraving of horse hair on the silver fetlock.

The other hoof, with silver mounts and a gold lid, is simpler in design and hallmarked 1840. However, the edge of the silver shoe and both sides of the gold lid are covered with engraved information, which establishes its history. This hoof was given by Angerstein to the Officers of the Brigade of Guards, also with a lock of *Marengo*'s hair. It is kept at the Officers Mess of The Queen's Guard at St James's Palace, where at luncheon every day it is placed in front of The Captain of The Queen's Guard.

Whether or not the skeleton and hooves of the horse at the two museums and St James's Palace are actually those of *Marengo*, or those of another imperial grey charger present at Waterloo, is an enduring question without a definitive answer. Nevertheless, French military history *savants* raised a considerable protest in 2021 when a plastic replica of the National Army Museum's equine skeleton was suspended on invisible wires over the Emperor's tomb in Les Invalides, as part of the bicentennial commemorations of his death. Curiously, the protest arose from the use of the skeleton installation as a modernist mobile, rather than from the plastic nature of the copy or the actual identity of the representation.

Marengo's front hooves

*   *   *

However, while Napoléon's horse was and remains the first key element in his later public profile, the Arab stallion could not be said to be reminiscent of Imperial Rome. For that, it is necessary to wait until the events of 18th Brumaire (9th November), 1799 when the curtain fell on the Directory and rose immediately on the Consulate. This was a new set, but one on which many of the old players were in new costumes and make-up.

Centre stage was the now short-haired figure of the First Consul, immaculate in a republican-red silk-velvet uniform. The first version of this dress, for all three Consuls, was double-breasted, with an open, turned-down collar, worn over a black stock and a white waistcoat. The edges, tail and collar of the coat, and the front of the waistcoat, were embroidered with Egyptian-style palmettes in gold thread. In some portraits of Napoléon, the jacket also has gold thread embroidery on the front and back seams of the sleeves, but this may have been artistic licence or a later embellishment. The Consuls are also depicted wearing a long sword-belt from the right shoulder, decorated with Roman motifs in gold and silver

The First Consul

Napoléon as First Consul,
after 1801

lace. In addition to these sword belts, when the three Consuls took possession of
the Tuileries Palace in late November 1799, Napoléon and his colleagues also
wore mid-blue silk sashes around their waists, although at the Installation of the
Council of State at the Petit Luxembourg Palace they had worn tricolour versions.

While the earlier red-velvet coat remained the same for all occasions, there
appear to have been three variants of the Consuls' uniform for the lower half of
the body: matching red velvet britches (*culottes*) with gold thread embroidery at

the knees, worn with white silk stockings and buckled patent-leather pumps, presumably for wear in the office; for more formal or ceremonial occasions, the red velvet was exchanged for white silk britches, embroidered down the front with gold thread work from waist to mid-thigh, and again worn with stockings and pumps; finally, for mounted ceremonial parades, the stockings and pumps were replaced with mid-calf-length, black patent-leather Hessian boots, with gold-laced tops and tassels.

Once in power, it did not take long for Napoléon to assert his superiority over the Second Consul, Jean Jacques-Régis de Cambacérès, and the Third Consul, Charles-François Lebrun, who almost immediately faded into the obscurity of titled but powerless positions. Perhaps in order to underline this concentration of the consular power in his hands, in late June 1800 Napoléon acquired a new dress coat and cloak, which he wore only on ceremonial occasions. The received wisdom is that these garments were given to him by the town council of Lyons, the centre of silk weaving in France, where he stopped off on 28th-29th June on his way back to Paris, after his crushing victory over the Austrians at Marengo in northern Italy. Far from being an unsolicited gift, it is far more likely that the silk-velvet coat and cloak were ordered by the First Consul to a specific design that was intended not only to differentiate him from the other Consuls, but also to send a subliminal message to his colleagues.

Far more richly embroidered with gold and silver thread than the earlier uniform, this new coat's embroidery featured an olive-leaf motif, the classical symbol for a victor. It was also single rather than double-breasted, with a stand up, open-necked collar, beneath which the black stock of the first uniform was replaced with a lace jabot. Over this coat, with its echoes of Austrian Court dress, was worn a matching red velvet cloak whose stand-up collar and turned-back facings were lined in heavily gold-embroidered white velvet.

Unlike the first iteration of the consular uniform, none of which appear to have survived, the First Consul's 1800 coat is now in the Napoléonic National Museum at the Château de Malmaison, albeit faded to the colour of rust. Its journey there was not guaranteed, however, for it travelled with the Napoléon to St Helena in 1815, where he gave it as dress material to the ten-year-old Hortense, daughter of General Comte Henri-Gatien Bertrand, Grand Marshal of the Imperial Household-in-Exile, and later the wife of the Second Empire Senator, Amédée Thayer. Fortunately, the young Hortense did not turn the consular coat into a dress. Instead, she returned with it to France and, sometime before her death in 1889, gave it to the ex-Emperor's great-nephew, Prince Victor Napoléon (known by his supporters as Napoléon V), from whose descendants it was bought by the Malmaison museum in 1979.

Napoléon's second consular uniform

Interestingly, until it was destroyed by fire in 1925, there was another heavily-embroidered coat (catalogued as belonging to the First Consul) on display at Madame Tussaud's in Baker Street. Only a grainy black-and-white photograph of this coat now exists, from which it is impossible to determine the colour. However, its gold embroidery was in a scrolling oak-leaf pattern, that was not used on either of Napoléon's consular coats. Further, the cut of the jacket and the use of the embroidery appears to be that of a French General of the period, so it may well have belonged to Napoléon and been worn by him during the Italian Campaign of 1800 in his role as a soldier, as opposed to that of his simultaneous role as First Consul. Evidence of the First Consul dressed as a General is provided by several contemporary paintings of the Battle of Marengo. These make an important point: during the Consulate, Napoléon dressed as a soldier for battle, but in Paris, in his role as a political leader, he dressed as a civilian. This was a distinction that would not survive the evolution of the French government from quasi-civilian rule to military dictatorship. Another reason for believing that the Madame Tussaud's coat was that of a General and not a Consul is evidenced by the fact that also in the collection was the blue uniform cloak that Napoléon had worn at the Battle of Marengo, which was used as his funeral shroud and bequeathed to his sone, the titular Emperor Napoléon II and former King of Rome. These two items of dress would usually have been kept together.

It is also worth noting, before the curtain drops on the Consulate and rises on the Empire that, as the Consulate progressed, the furniture in the First Consul's portraits became distinctly classical in style. The overall message of this is clear: Napoléon Bonaparte is no longer the wild, revolutionary General but a sober, modern-day version of the Consuls of Rome – at least for the time being.

*   *   *

The last act in the development of Napoléon's image falls into three scenes: his Coronation as Emperor of the French in 1804; a second Coronation as King of Italy in 1805; and the creation of his final and enduringly iconic image as the self-appointed role as 'the Master of Europe'.

Following plebiscite approval to make the Consulate permanent in 1802, the new constitution announced that the French people had named, and the senate proclaimed, Napoléon as First Consul for Life. It took only two more years, a further national plebiscite and yet another constitution for Napoléon to complete his Imperial Rome-inspired progression to becoming hereditary Emperor of the French on 18th May 1804. He had justified this move to permanent top billing for him and his heirs by exaggerating the threat posed by royalist assassins; and he then cemented it by eliminating a possible stand-in in the person of Duc Louis Antoine d'Enghien, a minor Bourbon Prince who was kidnapped in Baden, abducted back to France, tried for treason and executed by firing squad on 21st March 1804. Napoléon's Chief of Police, Joseph Fouché, said of d'Enghien's murder: 'It was worse than a crime; it was a blunder', as it contributed to the later Napoléonic wars.

The culmination of all of this was an extraordinarily lavish Coronation at Notre Dame Cathedral in Paris on 2nd December 1804, an event that even the film director, Cecil B deMille, would have had difficulty upstaging.

Perhaps the biggest surprise of this Coronation is that it took less than seven months for the preparations to be made, to designs by the young painter, Jean-Baptiste Isabey. He had started out as an *ancien régime* Court painter, but had more

Napoléon's Coronation, 2nd December 1804

Pope Pius VII (1742–1823)

recently been 'adopted' by Napoléon's wife, Joséphine, who doubtless took a cut of his fees, as she did with all the other government suppliers whom she patronised.

Isabey's designs were supervised by Napoléon and collated by Comte Louis-Philippe de Ségur, the Grand Master of Ceremonies, into *Le Sacre et le Couronnement de Napoléon*, known as the *Livre du Sacre*. This was the handbook for all aspects of the Coronation, and included in it were details and illustrations of an entirely new suite of imperial uniforms for all the Court functionaries. These official outfits, as will be seen later in the book, varied in colour and embroidery according to rank and appointment, from the Imperial Princes to the Pages: the gold-thread work alone must have kept an army of embroiderers at the workshop of Augustin-François-André Picot busy around the clock for months.

However, Isabey did not have a completely free hand in the designs for the Coronation, nor was there any attempt at the re-creation of a scene from antiquity – except, that is, with the central figure of the Emperor. For this was a great deal more than a ceremony, ladened as it was with subliminal messaging. It was, in fact, Napoléon's statement of intent, and one that his subjects, who were familiar with the iconography, could read with ease. For a start, it deliberately made no reference to the Bourbon Coronations, which had usually been held in Rheims Cathedral, nor was it a consecration. It was, instead, an entirely new ceremony consisting of two halves: a sacred first act, using mostly Roman Pontifical liturgy and presided over by Pope Pius VII, followed by a civil second act at the other end of Notre Dame. At no point was it ever the intention that the Pope would crown the Emperor, but it was important for the legitimacy of the event that it was conducted 'in the presence of God' and better still that God's presence was confirmed and endorsed by the Vicar of Christ, even though he withdrew to the sacristy before the profane second act.

Although, Napoléon's Coronation was Roman rather than royal in its format, the Imperial Impresario did not put the Senators into togas nor did he put the newly-created Marshals into Roman armour. Instead, their costumes for this most lavish of classical pageants were contemporary in their design, even if the dresses of their wives, caught high under an elevated bust, were straight from a classical frieze. Of the men involved in the ceremony, it was only the Emperor himself whose appearance was classical and it was ladened with visual messages, which were incorporated into every item that he wore: from the gold imperial laurel wreath on his head, in place of a crown and drawn from innumerable images of the Caesars, to the gold-laced bootees on his feet.

On the morning of the show, Napoléon set off from the Tuileries Palace with Joséphine in a new, eight-horse-drawn coach (now in the museum at Versailles) with an escort of Grenadiers à Cheval, of the newly formed Imperial Guard (formerly the Consular Guard and the equivalent of Britain's Household Cavalry), and the Imperial Guard's Gendarmes d'élite, who were tasked with the Emperor's security.

When he left the Tuileries, Napoléon was wearing his *petit habillement* (an order of dress roughly equivalent to English Court Full Dress). This comprised a gold-embroidered red velvet cloak, lined with gold-embroidered white velvet, and worn over a knee-length, single-breasted red velvet tunic, heavily encrusted with diamonds and a gold thread pattern of oak leaves,* from the shoulders of which hung the gold collar of the Grand Eagle of the Legion of Honour. Beneath was a white silk and gold-embroidered waistcoat. The outfit was completed with a white-and-gold-embroidered waist sash, white silk britches and stockings, gold-embroidered white gloves and pumps, a lace cravat, and a white plumed, black velvet bonnet with a diamond clasp to secure the feathers.

* The jackets of all the *petit habillement* worn at Napoléon's Court were either cut away from the waist, *à la française*, or closed to the knee, *à l'espagnole*. It is unclear from the *Livre du Sacre* why some were cut one way and some the other.

Napoléon in *petit habillement*

Napoléon in *grand habillement*

Napoléon's Coat of Arms

Joséphine in Coronation robes

Before entering Notre Dame, Napoléon exchanged the hat, shoes, cloak, jacket and waistcoat of the predominantly republican-red *petit habillement* for a classical-white *grand habillement*. This consisted of a long white-satin tunic, heavily embroidered with gold oak, acanthus and palm leaves and with a deep gold-bullion fringe. Added to this was a white-and-gold-bordered silk waist sash, a gold laurel wreath, and a gold-embroidered sword belt, at the end of which was an eagle-hilted sword in a diamond-encrusted scabbard on his left hip. Finally, before the actual crowning, a heavy crimson velvet mantle, weighing at least 80lbs, was donned to complete the *grand habillement*. This mantle had a lining, border and shoulder cape of Russian ermine, and was embroidered with golden bees and interlaced olive, laurel and oak sprigs surrounding the letter 'N'. According to the *Livre du Sacre*, the cost of the *grand habillement* was F(French Francs)74,118 (2020: £205,306) and the *petit habillement* F25,162 (2020: £69,698), excluding the diamonds for Napoléon's imperial regalia which cost a further F880,547 (£2,439,115).

These imperial symbols were also used in Napoléon's new Coat-of-Arms, on the carriage and on the various Coronation vestments and furnishings. Their selection had not been entirely straightforward, and was debated by the Conseil d'État a month after the proclamation of Napoléon's elevation to Emperor of the French on 18th May. Various heraldic devices were considered by the council, including a cockerel and an elephant, but finally the bee and the lion were chosen. The bees were a deliberate reference to the regalia of the Franco-Roman King Childeric I (437–481 AD), and neatly combined France, and the Roman Empire; they also signified immortality, resurrection, hard work and were (perhaps not accidentally) like an inverted fleur de lys. From this point on, bees were used extensively in every aspect of the new Empire style, alongside coroneted 'N's and the ubiquitous Roman eagles, which Napoléon had arbitrarily substituted for the lion less than a month after its use had been approved by the Conseil d'État.

As Napoléon was draped with his coronation mantle, the train of which was supported by the Second and Third Consuls, de Cambacérès and Lebrun, Joséphine was formally clothed with her own mantle. This she would never wear again, although it had a second and final outing when it was worn by Marie Louise of Austria, at her wedding to Napoléon in 1810. At the Coronation, this heavy mantle was borne by Joséphine's daughter, Hortense, Joseph's wife (the former Marie Julie Clary), and with considerable reluctance, by Napoléon's three sisters, Élisa, Pauline and Caroline, all of whom loathed the new Empress. So bad was this relationship that later in the ceremony, when Joséphine climbed a short flight of steps to be crowned, the Bonaparte girls stood on her train, hoping thereby to make her fall. Joséphine staggered, but did not entirely lose her balance, which was just as well as her *toute ensemble* had cost the French Treasury F63,368 (2020: £175,529).

Meanwhile, Napoléon's mother, the newly created Madame Mère, so disapproved of the event that she refused to attend and headed off to Rome. Her absence (and that of Napoléon's brothers, Joseph and Lucien) was later remedied in the official painting of the Coronation by Jacques-Louis David, in which she is given – entirely falsely – an elevated, central position, with the missing brothers depicted off to the left of the picture.

For the crowning itself, there was never any intention to use a Bourbon crown, even if all but that of King Louis XV had not been destroyed during the French Revolution. Instead, a new, medieval-style crown that harked back to the early years of the Holy Roman Empire, the so-called Crown of Napoléon (known as the Crown of Charlemagne for the occasion) was waiting on the altar. It is worth noting, at this point, that Napoléon treated the medieval Holy Roman Empire as a continuation of the classical Roman Empire, at least whenever it suited his script so to do. Anyway, as the Pope intoned the agreed blessing, Napoléon turned, removed his gold laurel wreath and crowned himself. Then he removed the crown, returned the infinitely more significant wreath to his head, and crowned the kneeling Joséphine with a small crown surmounted by a cross, which he had first placed on his own head. The Crown of Napoléon survived both the Restoration and the sale of the French royal regalia in 1885, and is on display at the Louvre Museum in Paris.

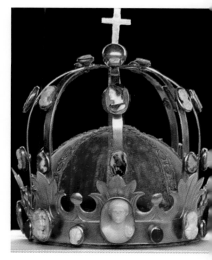

Napoléon's crown

Other than for the purpose of sitting for his portraits, Napoléon only wore his imperial *grand habillement* once more, when he presented new Imperial Eagles to his regiments three days after the Coronation. In 1842, both Napoléon's and Joséphine's Coronation mantles were bought by Madame Tussaud for £105 (2020: £12,142). This is a fraction of what they would be worth today, had they survived the 1925 fire. The tunic from Napoléon's *grand habillement* is preserved at the Musée Napoléon Prèmier at the Château de Fontainebleau. As for the gold laurel wreath, it was worn again on 26th May 1805 at Napoléon's Coronation in Milan as King of Italy, as will be described next, but although it was melted down at the Restoration of King Louis XVIII in 1819, nonetheless a number of leaves survive. Made by the goldsmith, Biennais in 1804, at a cost of F8,000 (2020: £22,160), the wreath was originally made up of fifty large leaves, forty-two detachable berries and twelve smaller leaves, set on an oval band and fixed at the back of the head by a pin. However, when he tried it on at its first fitting, Napoléon complained of the weight and six leaves were removed; these were later given by the goldsmith to each of his daughters. One of these leaves,

The Imperial laurel wreath

weighing a mere 10g and with a present-day scrap value of about £450, sold at a Paris auction in 2017 for £550,000; the whereabouts of the other five is unknown.

In addition to the leaves removed before the first Coronation, only one leaf from the actual wreath as worn in 1804 survives. Mounted on a snuff box, now on display at Fontainebleau, this leaf was given to Isabey by the Emperor, in circumstances that the artist recorded:

'At Saint-Cloud in 1805, before the departure for Milan [for Napoléon's Coronation as King of Italy], I was helping the Emperor as he tried on the [Italian] royal crown, which was supposed to go above the golden laurel wreath made for the Coronation in Notre-Dame. One of the leaves fell off. Just as I was about to give it to the Head Chamberlain, His Majesty said to me: "Keep it; it will make a good souvenir of your clumsiness".'

Since the establishment of the Consulate and then the French Empire, Napoléon had been at pains to construct a narrative that gave imperial Roman legitimacy to his role. Even after his Coronation as Emperor of the French, France was still technically a republic. So, on the face of it, Napoléon's decision on 17th March 1805 to appoint himself King of Italy was against the grain and, thereby, begs a number of questions.

For a start, why did Napoléon feel the necessity to change his 1802 title of President of the Italian Republic to King, while at the same time leaving it nominally a republic? Then why did he feel it necessary to organise a Coronation in Milan Cathedral on 23rd May 1805? And why did he not incorporate the territories into his growing empire, along with the rest of his conquests in central and northern Italy? There are a number of probable answers to these questions.

As to why he felt the necessity to place on his head the Crown of Lombardy there are two answers. First, his brothers Joseph, then Louis (on behalf of his son – and at that point Napoléon's designated heir – the infant Napoléon Charles), both refused the honour. Second, these territories had for years been administered by, or were within the orbit of, imperial Austria. By forming them into a kingdom, Napoléon's message to the peoples of the new Kingdom of Italy was clear: for generations you have been under the Austrian imperial heel, now you once again have your own kingdom. A second possible answer to this question was to keep the territory in line with developments in France. Created out of the Cisalpine Republic in 1802 when Napoléon was First Consul, it made logical if not constitutional sense to convert it into a kingdom when France became an empire.

As to the second question, not since the fall of the Roman Empire had Italy been unified, and at this time the southern half of Italy was – until 1806 – ruled by a Bourbon dynasty in Naples, and much of central Italy comprised the Papal States. The former was loosely allied to France's enemies, although the latter was *de facto* part of the French Empire while remaining *de jure* under the authority of the Pope. Nonetheless, given Napoléon's overarching plot, his decision to create himself King of Italy is at odds with the script.

Unlike the Coronation at Notre Dame, the one in Milan Cathedral on 26th May 1805 seems to have been less well organised and somewhat lower key. The only existing images show Napoléon wearing a *petit habillement*, similar to that worn *en route* to the Paris Coronation, but in green velvet, a nod to one of the Italian national colours. Flowers replaced the bees on his new green-velvet cloak (now in the Stibbert Museum in Florence), but he is shown wearing the same eagle-hilted Coronation Sword on his left hip that he had worn at the Paris ceremony. In some versions of the painting, Napoléon wears the imperial gold laurel wreath, but not in others. A very similar green velvet uniform, but without the laurel wreath, was worn by Napoléon's stepson, Eugène de Beauharnais, in his role as Viceroy of Italy, which can today be seen in the State Hermitage Museum collection in Russia.

In addition to the green *petit habillement*, a new carriage was made for the occasion, emblazoned on the door with the Iron Crown of Lombardy. After the ceremonies were over, this coach joined those in the Imperial Mews, before becoming permanently attached to the French Grande Armée on its travels. It

below, from left
Napoléon, King of Italy;
Eugene de Beauharnais
(1781–1824) as Viceroy of Italy

was seized in the wake of Waterloo and later ended up in the collection of Madame Tussaud, where it remained until the 1925 fire.

Following the portraits commissioned to commemorate the Milan Coronation, there are no images of Napoléon wearing the Italian green *petit habillement* and only a few in which he is depicted wearing one or other of three slightly different versions of the red *petit habillement*. After Waterloo, and before his exile on St Helena, all Napoléon's *petit habillements* were placed in the care of the Grand Master of the Wardrobe, the Comte de Turenne-d'Aynac. In his Will, the ex-Emperor bequeathed them to his brothers, Joseph and Louis. Only the cloak and jacket of the red *petit habillement* worn at his second marriage to Marie Louise of Austria in 1810 have survived and are now on display at Fontainebleau. So, for the most part after the Italian Coronation, while those around him blazed like over-decorated Christmas trees, Napoléon stood out by the simplicity of his dress. As with everything to do with the Emperor, this was no accident. In place of the velvets and gold braiding, from 1805 onwards Napoléon is almost invariably depicted in paintings and portraits wearing one of three simple uniforms.

These were the green and red uniform of a Colonel of the Chasseurs à Cheval of the Imperial Guard, worn when he was expecting to be mounted on a horse, typically during a campaign; the blue and white uniform of a Colonel of the Grenadiers à Pied of the Imperial Guard, worn when he knew that he was not going to be required to ride; and, occasionally, the blue and white uniform of the National Guard. The first two, therefore, were worn as circumstances demanded,

below, from left
Napoléon in uniform of the Grenadiers à Pied; Napoléon in the uniform of the Chasseurs à Cheval; Napoléon in a greatcoat

Napoléon in Russia, 1812

although there are some accounts that they were also alternated between week-days and weekends. In any event, as the memoirs of his valet record, these uniforms were ordered in very considerable quantities and delivered in bulk on the quarter days by the imperial tailor – Chevallier until 1812 and Lejeune thereafter.

With these iconic uniforms, Napoléon wore the riband, breast star and medal of the Legion of Honour, and one of a number of variants of his unembellished bicorne hat. All of these hats are believed to have been made by Poupard et Delaunay in the Palais Royal arcade, who supplied the Emperor with more than one hundred and fifty during his reign, at a cost of F60 each (2020: £166). Napoléon usually had twelve bicornes 'in service' at any one time, each of which had a lifespan of approximately three years. As with his shoes, the hats were broken in by his valet. A bicorne with traces of the Napoléon's DNA has recently come to light and is (at the time of publication) being auctioned by Bonhams with a pre-sale estimate of £100,000–150,000. This is in contrast to a Napoléonic bicorne with a good provenance, offered in a 1978 London auction with an estimate of £800–£1,200 (2020: £4,600–£7,000), which failed to sell, or the bicorne worn by Napoléon during the campaign of 1807, and at the signing of the Treaty of Tilsit on 7th July of that year. This was purchased for the equivalent of two guineas (2020: £185) on 26th August 1814 by Sir Michael Shaw Stewart Bt. He bought it from the Palace of Dresden, where the hat had been deposited by the Emperor's valet. It remained in the Shaw Stewart family until 2015, and then resold in 2021 for £962,298, as mentioned a few pages back.

Napoléon the icon

SAS handover to French Army, Tarbres, October 1945

So iconic are these bicornes that one of them was paraded symbolically, along with a cocked hat belonging to the 1st Duke of Wellington, at Tarbres in October 1945. The occasion was the handover of command to the French Army by ex-Chindit, Brigadier 'Mad Mike' Calvert, of two French-manned Squadrons of the Special Air Service Brigade. The Emperor's bicorne used in the ceremony is now in the collection of the Musée de l'Armée in Paris, and the Field Marshal's cocked hat is in the National Army Museum in London. Unfortunately for historical symmetry, the latter is not that famously used by Wellington to signal the General Advance at the Battle of Waterloo, but one of the same pattern worn by him in 1846.

The Imperial Impresario's wardrobe iconography was completed, as the weather determined, with a great coat. These were usually grey, although he also had them in blue and green. On winter campaigns he wore various velvet or cloth versions of these overcoats, all of which were trimmed and lined throughout with fur, one of which – along with a matching hat and waistcoat – was sold in 1819 at the Bullock Museum auction for a total of £6.15.0 (2020: £604).

With a few exceptions, the dominant image of Napoléon from 1805, in his ultimate role as Master of Europe, is as a simple soldier, often mounted on a pale-grey Arab charger. It is an image which, even two hundred years after the curtain dropped on the final act, is instantly recognisable. That is no mean achievement; but it is only a small part of the story.

Wellington signals the General Advance

CHAPTER TWO

OTHER STARRING ROLES

'A woman laughing is a woman conquered'

O SOONER HAD THE curtain fallen on the Consulate and risen on the Empire of the French, than a large number of the behind-the-scenes production team were given named parts and required to perform in front of the footlights. These new roles fell into two distinct but overlapping hierarchical categories, the first of which is the subject of this chapter. Top of the bill after the Emperor were the members of the newly-created Imperial Family, most of whom were granted the title of Imperial Highness, and required at Court ceremonies to wear the white *petit habillement* of an Imperial Prince or Princess.

For the men, this consisted of a white velvet jacket heavily embroidered along the seams, facings and edges with gold thread in a pattern of sunbursts, bees and laurel. Added to this was a matching cloak embroidered with gold bees and the star of the Legion of Honour, a gold-lamé sword belt, a white lace cravat, a black velvet hat with white feathers, and white velvet britches with silk stockings and black pumps.

In the leading female role, until it was re-cast in 1810, was Empress Joséphine. She had been born on 23rd June 1763, in the French colony of Martinique, into the sugar cane plantation-owning Tascher de La Pagerie family, whose wealth would be devasted by a hurricane three years after her birth. Christened Marie Josèphe Rose, she was known until her second marriage as Rose and identified as a 'Créole'. Although today this term implies that she was of mixed European and black Caribbean origin, at the time it was applied to people of French or Spanish ancestry who had been born in their countries' colonies in the West Indies and the Americas.

In a bid to restore the family's fortunes, Rose was taken by her father to Paris

opposite

Empress Joséphine (1763–1814)

Gillray cartoon of Barras,
Joséphine, Térésa Tallien
and Napoléon

in 1779 to wed Vicomte Alexandre de Beauharnais, the rich son of her paternal
aunt Edmée's lover, Marquis François de Beauharnais.

Despite producing two children, Eugène and Hortense, who later married
Napoléon's brother Louis in 1802, the marriage was not a happy one. By the time
the Revolution broke out in 1789, the de Beauharnais were living apart and Rose
was not grief stricken when, during the Reign of Terror, Alexandre was arrested
on 2nd March 1794. However, as the wife of an incarcerated royalist aristocrat,
his wife's position was precarious, particularly when she was imprisoned six
weeks after her husband. Her prospects of a long life did not improve when
Alexandre was executed on 23rd July. Fortunately for her, before Rose could
share Alexandre's fate under the blade of the guillotine, she and her fellow
prisoner, Thérésa Cabarrus, were released on 27th July through the intervention
of the latter's lover, the politician Jean-Lambert Tallien. He was married to the
notorious Térésa Tallien, a prominent political 'hostess' and *procureuse* during
the Revolution, and it was she who then guided Rose into the beds of a series of
senior revolutionary politicians, of whom the last and most important was
Vicomte Paul de Barras.

Then in late-1795 Rose met Napoléon. One story is that this occurred when
she went to see him, in his role as Governor of Paris, to thank him for returning
Alexandre's sword to Eugène. It is more likely that she was 'introduced' to him
by Madame Tallien. In any event, he quickly became besotted, re-named her
Joséphine and married her on 9th March 1796 in a civil ceremony for which he
was late. Her engagement ring, with a '*toi et moi*' gold setting of a pear-shaped

sapphire and a similar shaped diamond, was expensive when it was purchased by the impecunious General Bonaparte. It sold at auction in 2013 to an anonymous bidder for US$949,000 (£683,280).

The cost of the ring aside, Napoléon's family were appalled by his marriage. His deeply religious mother regarded her new daughter-in-law with distaste. Joséphine was six years older than her son, with two children of her own and a distinctly immoral reputation. His brothers thought that he could and should have made a far more politically advantageous marriage than Barras' ex-mistress; and his sisters felt that, whether deliberately or not, Joséphine made them look and feel like country bumpkins.

Talisman of Charlemagne

Two days after the wedding, Napoléon left to command the Army of Italy, from where he bombarded his new wife with love letters. While he was away, Joséphine began an unrestrained spending spree and quickly settled into a sexual affair with a young, amusing and handsome hussar called Lieutenant (later Captain) Hippolyte Charles. During this dalliance, the cavalryman acted as Joséphine's business manager in a series of corrupt military supply deals, intended to enrich him and offset her debts. The affair ended when, on his return from Egypt in 1798, Napoléon's brothers informed him of the reality of his marriage. In the ensuing Napoléonic explosion, further fuelled by Joséphine's acquisition in his absence of the run-down Château de Malmaison (along with an enormous repair and refurbishment bill), divorce was threatened. It did not, however, materialise at this point. The union could have been terminated on 24th December 1800, when a bomb in the rue Saint-Nicaise, Paris, designed to kill the First Consul *en route* to the opera, missed him but wrecked Joséphine's carriage behind his own. Although five people were killed, Joséphine survived unscathed and continued on to the opera house.

Although in the wake of the Hippolyte Charles affair their marital relations cooled, and there were constant rows about her spendthrift habits, Joséphine was, as already described, duly crowned Empress Consort of the French. By the time of the Coronation, she had her own extensive Household and a growing collection of jewellery, including a pendant known as the Talisman of Charlemagne. Given to Joséphine in 1804 by the Bishop of Aachen (then a part of France) during a visit to that city, it was a gift to thank Napoléon for the return of sacred relics stolen during the Revolution. Unlike Napoléon's Charlemagne crown in the Louvre, the talisman was genuine having been removed from Charlemagne's body when his tomb was opened in 1166 and thereafter preserved by the church. On Joséphine's death, it passed to her daughter, Hortense, who is depicted wearing it in 1834 in a portrait by Felix Cottreau. She in turn bequeathed it to Napoléon III, whose widow Eugénie eventually gave it to Cardinal Louis

The Divorce, 12th December 1809

Luçon, Archbishop of Rheims, who placed it in the Abbey of Saint-Remi, where it has been on display ever since.

By 1809, it was clear beyond any doubt that Joséphine was no longer capable of reproduction, and the growing brood of the Emperor's illegitimate offspring proved that no fault on that score lay with him. This, and the premature death in 1807 of her four-year-old grandson and Napoléon's nominated heir (Napoléon Charles Bonaparte, son Louis Bonaparte and Hortense), led inexorably to a tearful but amicable divorce; the civil marriage was annulled on 12th December 1809 and the religious contract on 9th January 1810.

Following the marital split, friendly relations were maintained. Joséphine was permitted to keep her title and her Household, granted a multi-million franc income, and was additionally created Duchesse de Navarre. Nonetheless, she was obliged to retire to Malmaison to cultivate her extensive collection of roses and other plants, and her even more extensive debts.

On 29th May 1814, shortly after showing her rose beds at Malmaison to Tsar Alexander I of Russia, and while her second husband languished in exile on

Elba, Joséphine died. On receiving the news of her death, Napoléon locked himself in his room for two days. On his own death bed seven years later, his last word was her name. That, however, was not her only legacy: some of her dresses and many of her bibelots are held in national and private collections; the rose garden at Malmaison has recently been restored to something like its original splendour; some of her jewellery is still worn by reigning Scandinavian royalty; a beautiful diamond and sapphire parure, which probably belonged to her and was then given to Hortense, is on display in the Louvre; the so-called Empress Joséphine tiara is in a Texas collection; and while Napoléon's legitimate bloodline came to end with the death of his son, the King of Rome, Joséphine's survived through Hortense, in the person of Napoléon III and, through Eugène, in the present royal families of Sweden, Norway, Belgium and Luxembourg. The last word on this curious relationship should, perhaps, lie with Joséphine: 'The only thing that ever came between us was my debts.'

Before moving the Imperial Family spotlight onto Joséphine's children and Napoléon's mother and his siblings, this is the moment to look at the re-casting of the female lead, just three months after Joséphine had left the stage, followed by the brief appearance of the juvenile lead.

Born Erzherzogin (Archduchess) Maria Ludovica Leopoldina Franziska Therese Josepha Lucia of Austria in Vienna on 12th December 1791, the future Empress Marie Louise was the maternal great-niece of the unfortunate Queen Marie-Antoinette (guillotined on 16th October 1793), and the eldest daughter of the man who in 1792 became the Holy Roman Emperor Francis I (from 1804, also Emperor Francis I of Austria). Brought up to hate the French, and the French Revolution in particular, she was an unlikely bride for Napoléon – but general understudies cannot be choosers when it comes to the recasting of a leading role. Concerned that Napoléon might marry Grand Duchess Anna Pavlovna of Russia, the sister of Tsar Alexander I, the Austrian Foreign Minister (later Chancellor and Prince) Klemens von Metternich moved swiftly and persuaded his employer that the eighteen-year-old Marie Louise was the girl for the part.

Napoléon was not particularly fussy about whom he married, providing she was impeccably royal and abundantly fertile: as he famously remarked, he was 'marrying a womb'. Nonetheless, he welcomed her to the stage via a proxy marriage in Vienna on 11th March 1810. This was followed by a civil and then a religious ceremony in Paris at the start of April, to mark which Napoléon gave his new bride a magnificent diadem, now in the Smithsonian National Museum of Natural History in Washington DC. As originally made, it had nine hundred and fifty diamonds (weighing 700 carats) and seventy-nine emeralds, although in the mid-1950s the emeralds were replaced with Persian turquoises.

Tsar Alexander I (1777–1825)

Empress Marie Louise (1791–1847) in Coronation robes

Empress Marie Louise and
Napoléon François Joseph
Charles Bonaparte (1811–1832),
King of Rome

He was less generous when it came to Marie Louise's imperial *grand habillement* robe, which was the one made for Joséphine. Other surviving relics of the marriage ceremonies include six huge, silver-gilt candlesticks and a crucifix made by Odiot for the high altar of the Salon Carré chapel in the Louvre, where the religious ceremony took place. These seven items, and some further pieces that have since been lost, had originally been intended as a gift for the Pope, but were quickly repurposed. Although not made specifically for the wedding banquet in the Hall of the Tuileries, the Emperor's 1,000-piece *Grand Vermeil* (silver gilt) service, given to him in 1804 by the City of Paris and made by Henri Auguste, was on display and in use on the high table. Only twenty-four pieces of this service survive and are at Fontainebleau.

Perhaps surprisingly, both parties took to each other immediately, Marie Louise telling her new husband on meeting him for the first time that he was much more attractive than his portraits. Napoléon, for his part, increasingly appreciated her honesty, thriftiness, lack of interest in politics and a rather shy nature (taken by some as haughtiness) – all of which were in sharp contrast to his previous wife. Better still, on 20th March 1811, eleven months after the ceremonies in Paris, she gave birth to a healthy boy, Napoléon François Joseph Charles Bonaparte, who was immediately created Prince Imperial and King of Rome. This second title was another deliberate reference to the Holy Roman Emperors, whose heir-designates bore the title 'King of the Romans' between 961 and 1756.

Twice appointed Regent while Napoléon was away on campaign, Marie Louise saw her husband for the last time on 25th January 1814, and was later forcibly dissuaded from following him to Elba after his first abdication. Under the terms of the treaties that exiled her husband, she was allowed to keep her French rank and titles, and she was created the ruling Duchess of Parma, Piacenza and Guastalla. She left Paris for Vienna on 23rd April with her son. There she remained there until 7th March 1816 when, obliged by the Allies in the wake of the Battle of Waterloo to leave the ex-King of Rome behind, she left for Parma. Arriving the following month, she ruled the duchies until her death on 17th December 1847, marrying twice more after Napoléon had died in 1821.

The King of Rome fared less well. Pampered almost to the point of absurdity in his infancy, at the tender age of three he was uprooted from France following his father's first abdication in 1814 and taken to Vienna. In 1818, his grandfather, Emperor Francis I of Austria, gave him the title of Herzog von (Duc de) Reichstadt (fervent Bonapartists ignored this title, named him Napoléon II and later gave him the posthumous nickname of 'L'Aiglon'). The ex-King of Rome spent most of the rest of his short life in Austria, dying of tuberculosis at the age of twenty-one on 22nd July 1832.

Duc de Reichstadt with sabre

Despite his insignificance to all but Bonapartists, many relics of Napoléon's only legitimate son survive including his heart and entrails, which are interred in separate urns in the crypt beneath St Stephen's Cathedral in Vienna. On the orders of Adolf Hitler, in 1940 the rest of L'Aiglon's body was transferred from Vienna to Les Invalides in Paris. However, a lock of his hair, given by Napoléon to his valet, Marchand, on St Helena and later sold in Paris, survived above ground until 1925, when it too was lost in the Madame Tussaud fire.

Many of L'Aiglon's less gruesome relics are in the Napoléonic collection of the French businessman, Bruno Ledoux, including his linen (in varying sizes), his christening robes, infant bonnet and bootees, a serinette music box, the remnants of a very large set of tin soldiers (known as the King of Rome's Gold Soldiers), some silver-gilt cutlery from a service made by Leonard Chatenet, and a cavalry sabre. There are also the unrealised plans for the little boy's own palace at Rambouillet, and numerous versions of his cot (one of which was also lost in the Madame Tussaud fire).

Eugene de Beauharnais

Of all of these mementoes of L'Aiglon, the most notable are the tin soldiers which, so legend has it, were gilded by Odiot and later used to convey secret messages (hidden in the base on tiny slips of paper or minutely engraved on the soldiers) between Vienna and Bonapartists in Paris. Recent examination has shown this to be a myth, although it confirmed that the now plain tin figures had indeed originally been gilded.

Definitely *not* a tin soldier was Eugène de Beauharnais, the only son of Joséphine and her first husband, Alexandre, and the adopted son (but not heir) of Napoléon. An able administrator, a very capable General in the field and an

Wedding of Eugene de
Beauharnais, 14th January 1806

Eugene's Viceregal
petit habillement

active Freemason, during the First Empire, Eugène was created an Imperial Prince, an Arch Chancellor of the (French) Empire, Prince de Venise, Duc de Frankfurt, and Viceroy of Italy, an appointment he held until Napoléon's first abdication in 1814, after which he retired from politics and the Army to live in Munich with his wife.

She was Prinzessin (Princess) Augusta Amalia Ludovika Georgia of Bavaria, daughter of King Maximilian I Joseph. Dressed in his Italian viceregal finery, in 1806 Eugène married her. Eleven years later, his father-in-law King created him the hereditary Duc de Leuchtenberg and Prince of Eichstätt, with the rank of Royal Highness. The seven children of the marriage took Joséphine's bloodline into that of the Swedish, Prussian, Portuguese, Brazilian and Russian royal and imperial families.

It was through the last of these connections, arising from the wedding of Eugène's youngest son, Maximilian, to Grand Duchess Maria Nikolaievna of Russia and their subsequent relocation to Saint Petersburg as fully-fledged members of the Russian Imperial Family, that Eugène's green velvet *petit habillement* as Viceroy of Italy came into the collection of the State Hermitage Museum. There it is held along with his violet velvet *petit habillement* as the Arch Chancellor of State, and some of his Napoléonic military accoutrements worn as Colonel of the Chasseurs à Cheval of the Imperial Guard, including a cross belt, sabretache and (for his horse) a leopard-skin shabraque. The whereabouts of Eugène's white Imperial Prince's *petit habillement* is unknown; indeed, only one is known to exist and that is in a Berlin collection, although its original owner has never been established but is thought to be either Joseph or Jérôme Bonaparte.

No such mystery surrounds the so-called Empress Joséphine Tiara. Despite its name, it was not made for the Empress, but was constructed in 1890 from diamonds given to Joséphine by Tsar Alexander I (on one of his visits to her at Malmaison after 1810) by August Holmström, who worked for the Russian Court jewellers, Fabergé. These loose stones had been bequeathed by Joséphine to Eugène, who passed them to his son, Maximilian, who in turn passed them to his son, George Maximilianovich de Beauharnais, 6th Duc de Leuchtenberg, who it was who had the stones set by Fabergé. This kokoshnik-style jewel then passed to George's son, Alexander. In exile and probably in great need of cash after the Russian Revolution, he sold the tiara at a Swiss auction in 1920 to King Albert I of the Belgians. He bought it for his wife, Queen Elisabeth (a former Duchess of Bavaria), who gave it to their younger son, Comte Charles de Flandres. Then, in a neat piece of historical symmetry, Charles left it to his sister, Queen Marie José of Italy, who in turn left it to her daughter, Principessa (Princess) Maria Gabriella of Savoy. It was she who ended the territorial, royal and imperial connections (but not the provenance) of the tiara by selling it at a Christie's auction in 2007 to the McFerrin Collection of Texas for US$2,071,389 (£1,491,400) including fees. That was double the low estimate, thereby demonstrating the value of a Napoléonic connection, no matter how tenuous.

Joseph Bonaparte (1768–1844) in white *petit habillement*

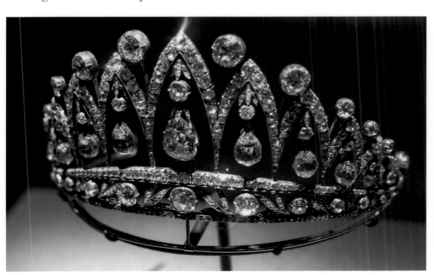

Empress Joséphine Tiara

Louis Bonaparte (1778–1846)

Joséphine's only daughter, Hortense, is the next into the limelight along with her husband Louis Bonaparte, the Emperor's younger brother. Their 1802 marriage was an arranged one (by the Emperor) and, as with Hortense's parents' marriage, it was not a happy union – although it produced three sons, the youngest of whom, Charles-Louis, would become Emperor Napoléon III.

When Napoléon created the Kingdom of Holland in 1806, he appointed his brother, Louis, to the throne. Hortense was a reluctant consort and the two lived separate lives in the Dutch royal palaces. So separate, in fact, that when Louis was forced by his brother to abdicate in 1810 and retired to Austria, Hortense returned to France and commenced an affair with the Comte de Flahaut, the illegitimate son of Talleyrand. In 1811 she went to Switzerland 'for her health', but in fact to give birth to his son, the future Second Empire statesman, Charles de Morny. He would be recognised as a half-brother by Napoléon III and, in 1862, elevated to a dukedom. Hortense's affair with de Flahaut ended in 1814, after which she moved permanently to Switzerland where she dedicated herself to good causes and musical composition.

Duc de Morny (1811–1865)

In addition to her jewellery and her bloodline, one of Hortense's most enduring legacies is *Partant pour la Syrie*, a patriotic song that she composed in 1807 to commemorate Napoléon's Egyptian Campaign. During the Second Empire, when *La Marseillaise* was regarded as too revolutionary, it became France's unofficial National Anthem. In a coloured engraving of the 1860s, the deceased Hortense is depicted allegorically singing the song to the deceased Empress Joséphine and her daughter-in-law, Empress Eugénie. Incorporated by the composer Camille Saint-Saëns into his *Carnival of the Animals* (Fossils), the *Partant pour la Syrie* remains in the musical repertoire of the French military.

Partant pour la Syrie

As to the rest of the Imperial Family cast, they all had their roles but only some of them have left a mark. Indeed, Napoléon's mother Maria-Letizia Bonaparte did her best in her lifetime not to have to step into the imperial theatre, let alone onto the stage. Married at fourteen in 1764, within nineteen years she had produced thirteen children of whom eight survived infancy. Widowed at the age of thirty-five, Letizia thereafter moved between Corsica, France and Italy until, in 1804, she relocated to Paris. Reluctantly accepting the title of Madame Mère, she declined to attend her son's Coronation; for most of his reign, she lived outside Paris and never attended the Imperial Court. On Napoléon's exile to Elba, as a dutiful mother Madame Mère followed him there and then returned with him to Paris for The Hundred Days.

However, after his second abdication she took herself, and the considerable fortune that she had thriftily amassed, to Rome where she bought a palazzo which she shared with her half-brother, Cardinal Joseph Fesch. He was a noted

Cardinal Joseph Fesch (1763–1839)

Joseph Bonaparte

collector of fine art, accumulating nearly 16,000 canvasses including works by all the great masters from the fourteenth to the eighteenth centuries. He also acquired the titles of Grand Almoner of France and Grand Chaplain of the Imperial Household, and the status of an Imperial Prince, a Peer of France, and a Prince of the Papal States. Letizia died in 1836, but Fesch lived for another three years, dying in 1839. He left the bulk of his collection, including works by Botticelli, Bellini and Titian, to the Fesch Museum at Ajaccio in Corsica, although the best pieces, including works by Raphael, Michelangelo and Leonardo da Vinci, were auctioned in 1845 and are now in national collections around the world.

Another fine art collector was Napoléon's oldest brother, Joseph Bonaparte. A political intriguer who plotted the Brumaire coup of 1795, he was married to Marie Julie Clary, elder sister of Napoléon's first love, by whom he had three daughters, only two of whom survived infancy. Following the French Army's invasion of Italy in 1805 and Napoléon's deposition of King Ferdinand IV of Naples, he appointed Joseph King of Naples and Sicily. From 1806 to 1808 Joseph was a popular monarch, who also found the time to father two illegitimate children with Maria, Contessa di Atri. His brief reign in southern Italy was followed by four years as a very unpopular King of Spain, the second throne on which he had been placed by his younger brother.

When that sinecure was ended by Wellington's advance on Madrid in 1813, Joseph comprehensively looted the Spanish treasury of its gold, and the royal palace in Madrid of its most portable contents. Some of the latter were placed in a large leather trunk that was strapped to the back of Joseph's carriage, which was captured in the immediate aftermath of the Battle of Vitoria by Captain Henry Wyndham of the Tenth Hussars, at the head of a party of the 14th Light Dragoons. Joseph managed to escape on a horse before he could be seized, albeit with nothing but the clothes he was wearing and a pocketful of diamonds, but the trunk he left behind was found to contain love-letters, engravings, drawings, manuscripts, and two hundred rolled-up canvasses.

Although most of these pictures were of a relatively small size, they represented works by some of the greatest artists of all time, including four pictures by Velázquez, and a painting by Correggio, *The Agony in the Garden*, which the then President of the Royal Academy, Benjamin West, said 'was worth fighting a battle for' and suggested that it should be 'framed in diamonds'. Were these not enough, the collection also included a painting by Sir Anthony van Dyck and works by Pieter Bruegel, Sir Peter Paul Rubens, Bartolomé Esteban Murillo and Girolamo Francesco Maria Mazzola (known as Parmigianino), to name but the best-known artists. Initially considered to be of significantly lesser value were three works attributed to the school of Tiziano Vecelli, known as Titian. However, after considerable research, these three paintings have more recently been attributed to the master himself.

As Henry Wyndham knew of Wellington's strong views on looting, he had the priceless canvasses sent back to General Headquarters. After the war, the Duke of Wellington wrote on three separate occasions to Ferdinand VII, the rightful King of Spain, informing him that his pictures had been recovered. Fortunately for the Duke's family, Conde (Count) de Fernán Núñez (the Spanish Minister in London) replied in 1816 to say:

'His Majesty, touched by your delicacy, does not wish to deprive you of that which has come into your possession by means as just as they are honourable'.

In addition to the haul of fine art in the carriage, Wyndham also found a richly-ornamented Sword of State, part of Joseph's Neapolitan royal regalia. This too was sent to Wellington, who in turn presented it to The Prince Regent, later King George IV.

While Wyndham marvelled at the haul of Old Master pictures that he had captured, his men had discovered an item in Joseph's carriage which probably caused them considerable amusement and Henry some distaste when it was shown to him. For inside the travelling carriage was a heavy, bulbous, single-handled, silver chamber pot, engraved with Joseph Bonaparte's coat of arms, a gift from his imperial brother, Napoléon (shown overleaf). In due course, this handsome piece of sanitary ware was first hammered flat by the 14th Light Dragoons, presumably for ease of transportation, and then taken back to England, where it was expertly restored to its former shape and christened 'The Emperor'. It then found its way into the Officers Mess silver collection of the 14th Light Dragoons. They in due course evolved into the 14th Hussars, then became the 14th/20th Hussars, and finally amalgamated (in an unconscious act of military-historical symmetry) with the Royal Hussars, themselves an amalgamation of Henry Wyndham's Tenth and the 11th Hussars, to become The King's Royal Hussars.

By way of a complete contrast to Joseph's imperial silver potty, there exist two further domestic trophies from his carriage. The first is a small silver beaker (shown overleaf) .This vessel, of thimble shape with a reeded rim and a gilded interior, was probably part of a larger *nécessaire de voyage*. As a label stuck to it asserts, it was acquired by Captain (later Lieutenant Colonel) Arthur Kennedy of the 18th Hussars and is still held in the collection of his lineal descendant, the publisher of this book. The second, a plain crystal tumbler in a protective wicker cover with lid, is now in a display cabinet in the Le Marchant Room at the Royal Military Academy Sandhurst.

Joseph's Sword of State

The Emperor

Joseph's tumbler

Meanwhile, at the fall of the First Empire in 1814, having briefly commanded the French Army retreating on Paris, Joseph left his wife in Europe and removed himself to the United States. There, with the diamonds that he had not left at Vitoria, he bought a large estate and fathered two more illegitimate daughters, this time by his mistress, Annette Savage (known, appropriately, as Madame de la Folie). In 1832, he moved to London and died in 1844 while on a visit to his estranged wife, who had by that time moved to Florence.

Of Napoléon's two remaining brothers to be considered here, Lucien Bonaparte and Jérôme Bonaparte, the former was the most revolutionary of all of the siblings and, with Joseph, planned and executed the Brumaire coup in his role as President of the Council of Five Hundred (the Lower House of the Directory). He then went on to be Napoléon's Minister of the Interior under the Consulate and was made a Senator during the Empire. However, he was unhappy with Napoléon's political direction-of-travel and rejected a dynastic marriage with Maria Louisa of Spain, the widow of the King Louis I of Etruria. In consequence, he was not made an Imperial Prince, refused to attend the Coronation and went into self-imposed exile in Rome in 1805.

In 1809, Lucien attempted to leave for the United States but was captured mid-voyage by the British Royal Navy and was later allowed to settle in England. There he stayed until his brother's first abdication in 1814, after which he travelled back to Rome where successive Popes created him Prince de Canino and Prince de Musignano. However, somewhat surprisingly, he joined Napoléon for The Hundred Days during which, for the first time, he was created an Imperial Prince. This, however, ensured his exile back to Italy on the Restoration, where he died in 1840 of stomach cancer, a fate he shared with his father, the Emperor and his sister, Pauline.

Of all the Bonapartes, Lucien was probably the most fertile (being father to thirteen legitimate children) and the most intellectual, being responsible for the

Lucien Bonaparte (1775–1840)

reconstitution of the Académie Française in 1803 and some notable archaeo-
logical excavations in Italy. These included the discovery of a statue of the
Emperor Tiberius and the 'Tusculum portrait', the only known contemporary
head of Julius Caesar, both of which conveniently but unintentionally comple-
ment the Roman theme of much Napoléonica.

By contrast with Lucien, Jérôme Bonaparte's career blossomed during the
First Empire and, uniquely, survived into the Second Empire. In another first for
the Bonaparte brothers, Jérôme's first wife was an American, whom he had met
in 1803 while in port in Baltimore with the French Navy. Unfortunately for the
young couple, Napoléon had other dynastic plans for his youngest brother and,
while Jérôme and his pregnant wife were in mid-Atlantic bound for France,
Napoléon annulled their marriage by Imperial Decree and pledged him to
Prinzessin Catharina of Würtemberg. Somewhat surprisingly, Jérôme went along
with this and, by way of imperial compensation, was created an Imperial Prince
and given the newly-created throne of Westphalia. Once in the equally-newly-
created capital of Kassel, Jérôme spent lavishly on expanding and refurnishing
the existing palace, renaming it the Napoleonshöhe, thereby incurring – to his
brother's considerable annoyance – as much expense as Napoléon had for his
considerably larger establishments in France.

Jérôme Bonaparte (1784–1860),
as King of Westphalia

For the Russian Campaign of 1812, Jérôme was given command of an Army
Corps but was reprimanded by his brother for travelling 'in State' with his entire
Court, which led him to return to Kassel in a sulk. There he remained until his
tiny kingdom was overrun by Prussian and Russian troops in 1813, after which he
fled to Paris then the USA. Like Lucien, he rallied to Napoléon's side during The
Hundred Days, but probably made a considerable contribution to defeat at
Waterloo by committing his entire Division in an all-day, unsuccessful attempt
to take the farmhouse of Hougoumont, held by the aforementioned Henry
Wyndham, amongst others.

In the wake of the Restoration of the French monarchy, Jérôme's father-in-
law created him Prince de Montfort and he moved to Italy, where he remained
until 1848 when his nephew became President of the Second French Republic.
Jérôme, who by this time looked remarkably like his brother the late Emperor,
was made Governor of Les Invalides in Paris and appointed a Marshal of France.
When Louis Napoléon became Emperor as Napoléon III, Jérôme served as
President of the Senate and was recognized as the heir presumptive until the
birth of Napoléon Eugène, Prince Imperial. Jérôme died in 1860 and is buried in
Les Invalides. There are far fewer relics of Jérôme and Lucien than their other
brothers, although the present Head of the House of Bonaparte (Napoléon VII)
is Jérôme's direct descendant.

Jérôme Bonaparte during the
Second Empire, c. 1852

In relation to Napoléonica, the same cannot be said of Pauline Bonaparte, Napoléon's second-eldest sister, whose bare-breasted image is seared into history's collective memory, thanks to a remarkably life-like marble statue of her by Canova, known as the *Venus Victrix*. However, long before she reclined for the sculptor in 1805, Pauline had first been married in 1797 to Napoléon's comrade-in-revolutionary-arms, General Charles Leclerc. He was not Pauline's choice but, nonetheless, within the year she had produced a baby boy who was christened, Dermide.

In 1801, Leclerc was sent by his brother-in-law, the First Consul, to supress a rebellion on the island of Sainte Domingue in the West Indies; Pauline and Dermide dutifully went with him. The expedition was a military success and Pauline quickly established herself as the 'queen of the island', in her role as the Governor General's wife. With the onset of the yellow fever season in the summer of 1802, Leclerc urged her to return to France but, in an oblique reference to her loathing of her sister-in-law, Pauline refused, saying: 'Here, I reign like Joséphine'. She may also have been reluctant to return to Paris because of all the horizontal fun she was having with Leclerc's soldiers. Her promiscuity probably resulted in her contracting yellow fever, which she and Dermide survived, but

Pauline Borghese (1780–1825)
in Canova's studio

the General and 25,000 of his men, including many of Pauline's lovers, did not.

By the beginning of 1803, Pauline, Dermide and the General's remains were back in France, where the two living members of the Leclerc family took up residence with Joseph Bonaparte in Paris. There she was required to observe strict mourning, which was not at all to her taste as it cramped, but did not eliminate, her extra-mural activities. This uncomfortable situation was not to last for long as Napoléon sought to re-cast his sister for a role in the French-occupied Italian 'theatre'. However, his attempts to send her up the aisle with the Duc de Lodi, Vice President of the Italian Republic (as it was still designated, failed. Instead, without Napoléon's consent as to timing and without giving up any of her lovers, she married a rich Roman Prince, Camillo Borghese, the 6th Prince di Sulmona. In November 1803, Pauline moved with her new husband and Dermide to the former's palazzo in Rome, although neither her son nor her tolerance of Camillo survived the move: Dermide died in August 1804 and Pauline was soon leading a semi-independent life.

Camillo Borghese (1775–1832)

In 1806, she separated from Camillo, leaving her husband and the Canova statue behind in the Palazzo Borghese, and moved to Guastalla in northern Italy, where she had been appointed sovereign Princess and Duchess by Napoléon. Once there, she quickly became bored with provincial life, and sold her territorial responsibilities to the neighbouring Duchy of Parma for six million Francs and the right to keep her princely title. This did not help her relationship with her brother, which soured further because of Pauline's overt hostility to his new wife, Marie Louise.

Despite this, Pauline was the only one of his siblings to console the temporarily exile in Elba, where she arrived bearing her entire wealth, having sold virtually everything she owned in order to support Napoléon in his adversity. Following her brother's second abdication, Pauline returned to Rome where, shortly before she died in 1825, she was re-united with her husband.

Wedding service by Biennais

Despite the 1814 liquidation of her assets, and the legacy of her louche reputation and the Canova statue, a number of portraits, some neo-classical jewellery and other memorabilia of Pauline survive. These include much of the 1,600-piece silver-gilt dinner service by Biennais, given to her on her second marriage by Napoléon, which is now in the Rockefeller Collection, and her Paris home, the Hôtel de Charost, which she sold in 1814 to the Duke of Wellington and has ever since been the British Embassy.

Of all Napoléon's sisters, the one best suited to the role assigned to her by him was Élisa Bonaparte. Passionately interested in both politics and the theatre, she was a faithful wife who bore her Corsican husband, Felice Baciocchi, four children. In 1805, Napoléon appointed her sovereign Princess of the strategically-

Elisa Bonaparte (1777–1820) and her daughter Elisa Napoléone (1806–1869)

important states of Lucca and Piombino, then in 1809 he made her Grand Duchess of the newly-re-established Duchy of Tuscany. In this second role, she had significantly less executive authority and found herself in opposition to many of her brother's policies in Italy, although she was in full agreement with his strategic aim of uniting Italy under his rule. This, and Napoléon's fiscal and military demands on Tuscany, led to considerable tensions with him. After the fall of the First Empire in 1814, Élisa was arrested and stripped of all her imperial titles, before being made Contessa di Compignano by the Austrian Emperor and permitted to live near Trieste. There she dedicated herself to archaeology, dying in 1820 of an illness contracted at one of her digs.

Last of the supporting players to be considered in this chapter are the double act of Caroline Bonaparte, Napoléon's youngest sister, and her cavalry-commander husband, the flamboyant Joachim Murat. Unlike most of her siblings, Caroline married for love at the tender age of eighteen in 1800, bore her husband four children, did not take lovers and only remarried fifteen years after her first husband had been executed in 1815.

Caroline Murat (1782–1839)

Created an Imperial Princess in 1805 and Grand Duchess of Berg and Cleves in 1806, her principal claim to fame is as Queen Consort of Naples from 1808 to 1815, during which reign she acted as a highly competent Regent for four separate periods when Murat was away. She also encouraged the design and manufacture of classically-inspired furniture, and – like her sister Élisa – took an active interest in archaeology. She also shared with all her sisters a loathing of Joséphine.

Most significantly, she supported her husband's disastrous decision to make a separate peace with the Allies in 1813, following Napoléon's defeat at the Battle of Leipzig, and then in 1815 to switch sides back to the Emperor, who nonetheless regarded him as a traitor. Rejected by his brother-in-law, Murat then attempted to re-take Naples only to be arrested, tried for treason and shot by firing squad on the orders of the rightful King of Naples, the Bourbon Ferdinand IV. In the wake of this tragedy, Caroline fled first to Austria then retired to Florence where, surrounded by other Bonapartes in exile, she died in 1839.

Marshal Murat (1767–1815)

As his many extant portraits show, Caroline's husband Joachim Murat was vain; not for nothing was he nicknamed the 'Dandy King'. He was also, like all good cavalry commanders, daring, brave, charismatic and – like many cavalry officers before and since – a bit dim. When he was shot through the cheek during the Egyptian Campaign of 1799, Napoléon remarked that it was the only time that Murat 'had opened his mouth to good purpose'. Napoléon's low opinion of Murat's grey cells notwithstanding, he recognised his brother-in-law's effectiveness as a leader of *l'arme blanche* on the battlefield and was grateful for his support during the Brumaire coup. In 1804, Napoléon made Murat a

Joachim Murat as King of Naples

Marshal of the Empire and gave him the slightly risible title of 'First Horseman of Europe'. Murat's subsequent appointments as Duc de Berg and Cleves, then King of Naples, did not stop him leading Napoléon's cavalry in the Peninsular War or in the Russian Campaign of 1812 and the German Campaign of 1813. His enforced absence at Waterloo is one of military history's great 'what ifs'.

In 1808, while fighting in the Peninsular War, Murat acquired and returned to France the sword of the French King Francis I, which had been lost to the Spanish in 1525 at the Battle of Pavia. Although that sword is not a piece of Napoléonica, except by association, several of Murat's own sabres are in national collections, including one from his reign in Naples, now in the Museo Napoleónico in Havana, Cuba, and another in the Royal Armoury in Naples, along with a ceremonial sword from his royal regalia. The sword on which was engraved 'Honour and Women', with which Murat hacked off the fingers of the Mameluke leader, Mustapha Pasha, while engaging him in single combat during the first Battle of Abukir in 1799, appears to have been lost. This is a pity as, should it ever come up for sale, it would undoubtedly fetch significantly more than two other cavalry sabres belonging to Murat, which each sold in 2014 for €289,000 (2021: £245,000).

The last words in this chapter are Murat's, spoken on 13th October 1815 as he faced a Neapolitan firing squad, with his hands and eyes unbound at his insistence. Brave and vain to the very end, he ordered: 'Soldiers! Do your duty! Straight to the heart but spare the face... *Fire!*'

Execution of Murat,
13th October 1815

CHAPTER THREE

PRINCIPAL and SUPPORTING PLAYERS

'Men are moved by two levers only: fear and self-interest'

 HILE MURAT WOULD not be the only one of Napoléon's stars to leave the stage in a hail of bullets, the majority of his principal and supporting players managed to survive; some even performed in future political productions, albeit with new scripts and costumes. Top of this cast list (after the Imperial Family) were the Grand Dignitaries of the Empire, whose purely ceremonial appointments were in addition to their executive roles. To complicate matters, most of these Grand Dignitaries were also Imperial Princes, but not all of the Imperial Princes were Grand Dignitaries. As this chapter illustrates, dress and uniforms were an important part of the imperial tableau and, as a general rule, Napoléon expected the Imperial Princes to wear their white velvet *petit habillement* at Court functions, although some of them apparently preferred not to. Fortunately for them, Jean-Baptiste Isabey, as wardrobe-master-in-chief (although he was not Grand Master of the Wardrobe), also designed for each of the Grand Dignitaries a role-specific and colour-differentiated velvet *petit habillement*.

The uniform colour coding of the Grand Dignitaries appointed in 1804 was:

Grand Elector of the Empire (Joseph Bonaparte): poppy red

Grand Constable of the Empire (Lucien Bonaparte): dark blue

Arch Chancellor of the Empire (Jean Jacques-Régis de Cambacérès): mid-blue

Arch Treasurer of the Empire (Charles-François Lebrun): black

Arch Chancellor of State of the Empire (Eugène de Beauharnais): violet

Grand Admiral of the Empire (Joachim Murat): green

To differentiate these uniforms from the Imperial Princes' white velvet *petit habillement*, which were embroidered with gold and silver laurel leaves, the star

Jean Jacques-Régis Cambacérès (1753–1824) in the *petit habillement* of Arch Chancellor of the Empire of the Legion of Honour, bees and sunbursts, the Grand Dignitaries' uniforms were embroidered in gold thread featuring foliage, oak leaves and acorns on the jacket, bees on the cloak and the star of the Legion of Honour on both.

The list of Grand Dignitaries was lengthened in 1805, when Napoléon appointed his half-uncle, Cardinal Joseph Fesch, as Grand Almoner; in this role Fesch wore the ecclesiastical robes of his clerical rank. The list was increased again in 1807, when the Emperor elevated to Grand Dignitary status Prince Charles Maurice de Talleyrand-Périgord, as the Vice Grand Elector of the Empire, and Marshal Louis-Alexandre Berthier as the Vice Grand Constable of the Empire.

Charles Maurice de Talleyrand-Périgord (1754–1838)

The club-footed Talleyrand had been born into an aristocratic family of the *ancien régime*, became a priest in 1779 and, under Louis XVI, served as a Deputy of the Estates General. Deftly switching sides during the Revolution, Talleyrand became a Member of the National Constituent Assembly, was actively complicit in the Brumaire *coup d'État* and, under Napoléon, he was created sovereign Prince de Benevento in Italy. Politically if not physically nimble to the very end, he served (on and off) in French governments before, during and after the First Empire as Minister of Foreign Affairs. An unscrupulous and slippery political operator, Talleyrand was memorably referred to by the Emperor as 'a shit in a silk stocking'. From a contemporary portrait, it appears that his *petit habillement* as a Grand Dignitary was bright red and cut *à l'espagnole*.

Marshal Louis-Alexandre Berthier was Napoléon's Minister of War, Chief of Staff and one of the original eighteen Marshals of the Empire. In addition to his appointment as Vice Constable of the Empire, he was created Duc de Valangin and sovereign Prince de Neuchâtel in 1806, and Prince de Wagram in 1809. A superb staff officer, he opposed the Russian Campaign and, on Napoléon's return from Elba, committed suicide two weeks before the Battle of Waterloo by throwing himself out of a window. He does not appear to have had a specific Grand Dignitary's *petit habillement* as Vice Constable, being depicted in contemporary pictures wearing that of either the Grand Master of the Hunt or a Marshal of the Empire.

Charles-François Lebrun (1739–1824) in Arch Treasurer's *petit habillement*

The list of Grand Dignitaries was further added-to in 1809 with the appointment of Prince Camillo Borghese as Governor General of the Departments Beyond the Alps. His uniform for the role was a dark blue velvet *petit habillement*, as depicted in a full-length portrait by Gérard, now (despite Italian export licence objections) in the Frick Collection, New York; and Élisa Bonaparte, as Grand Duchess of Tuscany.

Finally, Charles-François Lebrun, since 1808 the Duc de Piacenza, was given in 1810 the added Grand Dignitary appointment of Governor General of the

Departments of Holland. From contemporary portraits, Lebrun does not appear to have worn an honorific-specific uniform in addition to his Arch Treasurer's black *petit habillement*. However, he is depicted in a post-Restoration portrait by Robert Lefèvre in the Court uniform of a Peer of France, in which his blue velvet coat is less richly embroidered than his Grand Dignitary jacket, and his matching cloak is ermine rather than white-silk lined.

*   *   *

Positioned in the Imperial cast list between the Grand Dignitaries of the Empire and the Grand Officers of the Imperial Household (see below) were the Marshals of the Empire. This was a re-instatement in 1804 of the old Bourbon title that had been abolished in 1793, but with the substitution of 'Empire' for 'France', and batons decorated with eagles rather than fleurs-de-lys. Officially, the title 'Marshal of the Empire' was a civil title not a military rank, although, in their military uniforms, Marshals wore four stars on their epaulettes, rather than the three worn by a General.

To highlight their intermediate position between the Grand Dignitaries and the Grand Officers of the Imperial Household, the Marshals' *petit habillement* was virtually the same as that of the Grand Constable, being made of dark blue velvet with the same amount of gold embellishments. However, the embroidery featured oak leaves and acorns only, as on the Marshals' military tunics, which was a subtle but important difference.

Needless to say, some of the Marshals, of whom there were originally eighteen (increased by a further twelve appointments between 1807 and 1815), were

far left
Marshal Ney (1769–1815)

left
Petit habillement jacket of a Marshal of the Empire

Execution of Ney,
7th December 1815

also Imperial Princes (Joachim Murat), Grand Dignitaries (Joachim Murat
again) or Grand Officers (Berthier), and all of them were Generals. Their uniform
cupboards – Murat's in particular – must have been fit to bursting. Despite this,
only the *petit habillement* of Marshals Michel Ney, Louis-Nicolas Davout, Jean
Lannes and Nicolas Oudinot, all cut *à l'espagnole*, still exist in French public
collections.

Michel Ney, created by Napoléon Duc d'Elchingen and Prince de la Moscowa
(Moscow) in 1812, started life as a civil servant under the *ancien régime*, but then
enlisted in a hussar Regiment in 1787. There he was obliged, as a non-aristocrat,
to start in the ranks. However, the fall of the monarchy led to Ney's swift acquisition of an officer's commission and, by 1799, he was a General of Division (Major
General) with a reputation for bravery and 'cavalry dash'. Known by his men as
Le Rougeaud on account of his red hair, and as *Brave des Braves* by the Emperor, he
distinguished himself as a commander of cavalry in all of Napoléon's campaigns
in which he fought, up to 1814.

Thereafter, he showed questionable political, personal and military judge-
ment. The spokesman for the so-called 'Marshals coup' that forced Napoléon's

first abdication, Ney swore allegiance to Louis XVIII and, when Napoléon landed at Golfe-Juin at the start of The Hundred Days, he promised the king to bring his former master back to Paris 'in a cage'. Instead of which, he went over to Napoléon, made some fatal errors in his command of the Army of the North's left wing at the Battle of Waterloo, and was later arrested, tried for treason and shot by firing squad on 7th December 1815 in circumstances that echoed the execution of Murat nine weeks earlier. Like Murat, Ney was unbound and gave the order for his own dispatch with the words:

'Soldiers, when I give the command to fire, fire straight at my heart. Wait for the order. It will be my last to you. I protest against my condemnation. I have fought a hundred battles for France, and not one against her ... Soldiers, fire!'

In addition to his *petit habillement* preserved in the Musée de l'Armée in Paris, a rare gold snuff box given to Ney by the Emperor sometime between 1808 and 1814 lies in a display case in the Green Howards Museum in Richmond, North Yorkshire. It was taken from Ney's carriage after Waterloo by Captain (later Colonel) William Cameron of the 1st or Grenadier Regiment of Foot Guards. He gave it to his son, who served in the Green Howards, and in 2006 a descendant presented it to their museum.

Ney's snuff box

Louis-Nicolas Davout (or d'Avout), created Duc d'Auerstaedt and Prince d'Eckmühl in 1808, so started his career in the Army of the *ancien régime* at the same military school (Brienne-le-Château) as Napoléon. He was commissioned in 1788 as a Sous (Second) Lieutenant into a cavalry Regiment but at the outbreak of the Revolution quickly embraced its principles, and rose to command a Brigade in 1793.

Unfortunately, his connections to the nobility led to his suspension from the active list during The Terror but after the fall of Robespierre he was re-instated. He quickly became a protégé of Napoléon, who arranged his marriage to Pauline Bonaparte's sister-in-law, Aimée Leclerc, and assured his rise to the top as the youngest of the eighteen Marshals to be appointed in 1804. A strict disciplinarian, Davout acquired the nickname of 'the Iron Marshal' and the reputation as one of Napoléon's most trustworthy field commanders, although the Emperor criticised him heavily for his command of the rear guard during the 1812 retreat from Moscow (in which he lost his baton), and replaced him with Ney.

Unlike Ney, Davout refused to transfer his allegiance to Louis XVIII in 1814 and went into retirement. In 1815, he re-joined the Emperor, was appointed Minister of War, and was tasked with reconstituting the Grand Armée. Left at his desk in Paris, he was not at the Battle of Waterloo and his absence may have contributed to its outcome. Following the second abdication, Davout again retired, although he campaigned against the execution of Ney. This, and his

Marshal Davout (1770–1823)

Death of Marshal Lannes,
31st May 1809

loyalty to Napoléon, did not endear him to Louis XVIII, who stripped Davout of his rank and titles, only to restore them to him in 1817 six years before the Marshal's death from natural causes in 1823.

The military career of Jean Lannes, created Duc de Siewierz in 1807 and Duc de Montebello in 1808, resembled more closely that of Ney than it did Davout, for he was of relatively humble birth and also had to rise to high command through the ranks. He appears, however, to have combined their best characteristics: bravery and military competence. A personal friend of Napoléon who, even after 1804, allowed Lannes to address him with the familiar '*tu*', he is still rated as one of the Emperor's most talented Generals. Sadly, he died of appalling wounds in 1809 after being struck by a stray cannon ball during a lull in the Battle of Aspern-Essling in Austria. He was aged just forty. His early demise creating another of history's 'what ifs'.

Nicolas Oudinot, created Conte Oudinot in 1808 and Duc de Reggio in 1810, is best known for sustaining thirty-four wounds during his military career. Like Ney and Lannes, his early service in the royalist Army of Louis XVI was blighted by his non-aristocratic lineage, but during the Revolution he was swiftly promoted to a General of Brigade. He continued to prosper under the wing of General André Masséna, rising to Inspector General of Infantry in 1804. He was not, however, in the first creation of Marshals, having to wait until after the Battle of Wagram in 1809. Following Napoléon's first abdication, Oudinot threw in his lot with Louis XVIII and did not defect back to Napoléon during The Hundred Days. This ensured him a Bourbon peerage, further Army commands and the governorship of Les Invalides from 1842 to 1847, where he died in office aged eighty.

Marshal Oudinot (1767–1848)

*   *   *

Next on the cast list in Napoléon's theatre of power were the Civil Grand Officers of the Imperial Household. Unlike the Grand Dignitaries and the Marshals, they had jobs attached to their titles. However, to demonstrate their subsidiary status to those exalted beings, the embroidery on the Grand Officers' *petit habillement* featured palm trees (the new symbol of the Imperial Household) surrounded by oak leaves, acorns, and laurel fronds in *silver* thread, with the following colour coding of the velvet:

Grand Chamberlain – scarlet
Grand Marshal of the Palace – amaranth red
Grand Master of Ceremonies – violet
Grand Equerry – light blue
Grand Master of the Hunt – green

It is worth noting at this point that, when trying to identify the rank or appointment of a wearer of these uniforms, while all Court functionaries wore the same colour of velvet and pattern of embroidery as the head of their department, only the jackets of the Imperial Princes, the Grand Dignitaries, the Marshals of the Empire and the Civil Grand Officers had embroidery on the front and back seams of the sleeves. The embroidery on the cloaks and jackets of lesser ranks diminished in size and extent according to their rank.

Petit habillement of a Grand Marshal of the Palace

The most senior of the Grand Officers was the Grand Chaplain, a role assigned to Cardinal Joseph Fesch. The job involved the supervision of all the religious affairs of the Imperial Household from daily services, masses, weddings, baptisms and funerals, to delivering Grace before every meal. As with his other imperial roles and appointments, Fesch did not have a special uniform as Grand Chaplain, but wore his various ecclesiastical vestments when on duty.

The first Grand Chamberlain of the Empire was Talleyrand, who was given the office in 1804 in addition to his duties as Foreign Minister and his rank as a Grand Dignitary. This appointment was seen by many as a way of putting Talleyrand into a subservient position, in which he would be responsible for overseeing the everyday operation of the Imperial Household. In practice, most if not all of the Grand Chamberlain's duties, as with the other Grand Officers, were delegated to his extensive staff of officers, adjutants and assistants. These included the First Chamberlain, the Master of the Wardrobe, and a bevy of lesser chamberlains, ushers, and valets of the bedchamber.

Having been elevated to a Grand Dignitary in 1807, two years later Talleyrand was suspected by Napoléon of treason, removed from office and replaced as Grand Chamberlain by Comte Pierre de Montesquiou-Fezensac. Like Talleyrand, he was an aristocrat of the *ancien régime* but, unlike his club-footed predecessor, was willing to get fully-engaged in the duties of his new department with many of which he was already familiar, having been First Equerry to Louis XVI's brother, the Comte de Provence, later King Louis XVIII.

The Grand Marshal of the Palace was responsible for all the military personnel within the imperial palaces. He also supervised the upkeep and furnishing of the buildings, and food, heating, lighting, silver, linen and servants' liveries. This task was given to another ex-ranker, General Géraud Christophe Michel Duroc, created Duc de Friuli in 1808, who was believed to be one of Napoléon's closest friends. Sadly, for the Emperor, Duroc – like Lannes – was killed by a cannon ball while on active service in Silesia in 1813. After a seven-month interlude, during which General Armand de Caulaincourt filled the post before becoming Foreign Minister, Duroc's more permanent replacement as Grand Marshal of

Comte Pierre de Montesquiou-Fezensac

Death of Marshal Duroc, 23rd May 1813

the Palace was General Comte Henri-Gatien Bertrand. He alone amongst the Grand Officers, stayed in the role during his master's exiles on Elba and St Helena. His *petit habillement*, cut *à la française*, is preserved at the Musée de la Mode de la Ville in Paris. Bertrand's staff of office – the only one of a Grand Officer to have survived – is held at the Musée-Hôtel Bertrand in Châteauroux.

Next came the Grand Master of Ceremonies, in the person of the *ancien régime* aristocrat, Comte Louis-Philippe de Ségur. He held the job between 1804 and 1814, and again in 1815. In addition to the work implicit in his job title, he was responsible, for organising the presentation of foreign ambassadors. Unusually for a Grand Officer, de Ségur was an intellectual, a member of the Académie Française, and had a serious interest in philosophy and history. The latter interest came in very useful when he was engaged in organising the protocols and etiquette of the new Court, although his numerous tasks forced him to suspend publishing his historical works and his memoirs, something which he was able to recommence after the Restoration of the monarchy in 1815.

The Grand Equerry was responsible for the Emperor's couriers, travel arrangements, and everything associated with them, from the stud farm at Saint Cloud to the stables and the growing collection of carriages. The man appointed in 1804 to hold this important post was the aforementioned Armand-Augustin-Louis de Caulaincourt, an aristocrat from Picardy and the youngest of the Grand Officers at a mere thirty years of age. A soldier since he was fourteen,

below, left to right

General Henri Gatien Bertrand (1773–1844); General Armand-Augustin-Louis de Caulaincourt (1773–1827); Comte Louis Philippe de Ségur (1753–1830)

Caulaincourt attained the rank of a General of Division, and was created Duc de Vicence, in 1808. In addition to his duties with the imperial horseflesh he was sent as French Ambassador to Russia in 1807, when he became very friendly with Tsar Alexander I. He also served as Master of the Horse in the Russian Campaign of 1812 and as already mentioned was an interim Grand Marshal of the Palace between the death of Duroc and the appointment of Bertrand. During The Hundred Days, he served as Napoléon's Foreign Minister and Master of the Horse, and was, in consequence, proscribed during the Restoration. He was saved from execution by the intervention of the Tsar, and went into retirement. Like Napoléon, he died of stomach cancer, although not until 1827. De Caulaincourt is now best known for his memoirs, which he based upon contemporaneous notes of events, particularly during the Russian Campaign, and his conversations with the Emperor. It is known from German officers interviewed after the Second World War, that de Caulaincourt's insights into the problems Napoléon encountered in Russia were essential reading for Field Marshal Günther von Kluge, commander of Army Group Centre during Operation Barbarossa, Germany's invasion of the Soviet Union in 1941.

Last of the Grand Officers was the Grand Master of the Hunt, whose initial duty was to re-establish courtly hunting and shooting as it had been under the *ancien régime*. This was a clear case of Napoléon's willingness to compromise his imperial Roman theme when it suited him. Although an indifferent rider and

right
Marshal Berthier (1753–1815) as Grand Master of the Hunt

far right
Joseph Bonaparte in Senator's *petit habillement*

Château de Chambord

a poor shot, the Emperor recognised the power of organised field sports as part of his imperial Court 'theatre'. The man tasked with the job was Marshal Louis-Alexandre Berthier, who has been considered earlier in connection with his other imperial roles and duties. Napoléon's choice of Berthier as Grand Master of the Hunt was not, however, based upon the Marshal's undoubted skills as a staff officer but rather on his knowledge of the former royal hunting grounds. This he had acquired through his father, who had conducted a survey of these properties for Louis XVI. Along with his green *petit habillement* cut *à la françaises* (now on display in the Musée de l'Armée in Paris), Berthier also acquired the estate and Château de Chambord, the largest building in the Loire valley, and the forest and Château de Grosbois to the east of Paris

*   *   *

Of the subsidiary roles within the Imperial Court and the government, those Senators and Ministers who did not rank as Grand Officers wore the same blue velvet as the Grand Constable and the Marshals of the Empire, but the silver embroidery on their coats was of a floral pattern for the former, and a laurel and oak leaf pattern for the latter, and did not extend to the seams of their sleeves. Senators and Ministers were further distinguished as of subsidiary rank by wearing britches of the same material as their jackets.

Viewed *en masse* at a ceremonial event, the cast and crew of Napoléon's imperial production presented an awe-inspiring display of kaleidoscopic colours that outshone anything seen before or since. That, of course, was the intention. However, there was far more to the Imperial Impresario's 'theatre' than just those featured on the playlist.

French First Empire civil uniforms

CHAPTER FOUR

PROPS

'Men are ruled by toys'

 HE PREVIOUS CHAPTERS have focussed on the principal players in the imperial drama that unfolded in the early years of the nineteenth century and, along the way, looked at the dazzling array of non-Roman costumes in the Empire's wardrobe department. However, while the status, ranks and dress of Napoléon's Court may at times have been in danger of veering off the imperial script, there were no such perils lurking in the props department, wherein were to be found the most iconic of the symbols of Napoléon's imperial production: the regimental Eagles, the Legion of Honour and other Orders, and the batons of the Marshals of the Empire.

In order to fully understand the significance of the Eagles, it is necessary to go back to the classical source, which was the Legions of the Roman Republic and Empire. From 104 BC, every Roman Legion carried at its head a standard, known as an *aquila* (Latin for 'eagle'). This took the form of a pole, carried by a lion-skin-clad soldier known as an *Aquilifer* (a rank immediately below that of a Centurion). At the top of pole was a gilded eagle with outstretched wings, usually surrounded by a laurel wreath, and perched on a 'Jupiter's spindle' above four lightning bolts. The *aquila*, which was always closely guarded, acted not only as the rallying point for the Legion's soldiers, but also as the spirit of the Legion. Possessed of an almost religious significance, the loss of an *aquila* in battle was considered a disgrace, which sometimes led to the Legion's disbandment. Recovering them from the enemy led to some epic encounters. In the four hundred and fifty years between 73 BC and 378 AD, between twenty-six and thirty

opposite

Sergeant Charles Ewart captures the French Eagle in Richard Ansdell's *The fight for the standard*

Roman Aquilifer

1804-pattern Eagle Standard

1812-pattern Eagle Standard

Napoléon bids farewell to
the Old Guard, Fontainebleau,
20th April 1814

aquilae were temporarily or permanently lost by the Legions of Rome. No one can be certain of the actual count.

The use of such quasi-religious symbols, embodying the *esprit* of a regiment, evolved in the armies of the Middle Ages into flags or *drapeaux*, variously known from the fifteenth century onwards as Colours (infantry), Standards (heavy cavalry) or Guidons (light cavalry). In the armies of the French Bourbon monarchs, the design of such regimental *drapeaux* varied greatly, but all featured the white Cross of France and the fleur-de-lys.

All these symbols of the *ancien régime* were swept away by the French Revolution, along with the existing infantry regimental structures of the Bourbon Army. In their place Demi-Brigades were established in 1793, each consisting of three battalions with its own Colour. In 1804, these units were replaced under the French Empire by Department-based-and-recruited regiments, each consisting of six battalions, with a single Colour carried by the 1st Battalion, although they were later carried by every battalion.

These Colours were known as *Aigles* or Eagles and comprised four elements: a blue pole, at the top of which was the eponymous eagle; this was attached to a plinth on which was the regimental number or, in the case of the Imperial Guard, '*Garde Impériale*'; below the plinth were embroidered fabric streamers, known as '*le cravat*'; and attached to the pole was the *drapeau* itself, the design of which was based until 1812 on the Colour of the 1st Demi-Brigade. This had a white diamond in the centre, with the corners filled in (from clockwise top left) alternately

in red and blue; the name of the Regiment was written in gold on the obverse; and the words *Valeur et Discipline*, together with the Battalion number, on the reverse; finally, the regiment's number was written in gold in the four corners.

In 1812, a new pattern of regimental *drapeau* was authorised. This used the tricolour fringed in gold, with various regimental and imperial devices forming a frame around the central gold writing. The obverse bore the name of the regiment, while on the reverse were listed its battle honours. However, as only the actions in which the Emperor himself had participated were recorded in this way, some regiments had nothing on the reverse of their Colours.

1804-pattern of Eagle

The Colours of the Imperial Guard were subject to the same regulations, with the addition of either grenades (for Grenadiers) or hunting horns (for Chasseurs) in the centre and at the corners. The French Cavalry of the Line Cuirassiers, Carabiniers and Hussars all carried square Standards, while the Dragoons, the Lancers and Chasseurs à Cheval, as well as the Horse Artillery, all had swallow-tailed Guidons.

The most important element of these various *drapeaux* was the gilded eagle finial, which was about ten inches high and deliberately based on the Roman Legion's *aquila*, the eagle having been arbitrarily substituted by Napoléon in mid-1804 for the lion chosen by the Conseil d'État. The original model for the Napoléonic Eagles, of which there were in total 1,100, was sculpted by Antoine-Denis Chaudet, then cast in bronze and gilded in the workshop of Pierre-Philippe Thomire. In recognition of their exploits on the battlefield, some regiments were later honoured by Napoléon with a gold laurel wreath which was fixed around the icon's neck.

1815-pattern of Eagle

Following Napoléon's first abdication, the newly restored Louis XVIII commanded that all the 1804 Eagles be destroyed, although some were hidden and so survived. Then, during The Hundred Days, Napoléon ordered that new Eagles were to be cast and Colours, Standards and Guidons manufactured. However, because of the lack of time, many of the replacement *drapeaux* were merely painted canvas or silk; and because of the loss of the original mould and the need for speed, the replacement finials, of which there were 292, were of an inferior quality and can be recognised easily by their closed beaks.

Before any of this was to happen, on 5th December 1804 the first variants of the Eagles and their *drapeaux* were presented by Napoléon to his regiments in a grand ceremony held on the Champ de Mars, with the École Militaire acting as a backdrop. Napoléon made a rousing speech to his troops in which he told them: 'Soldiers! Here are your flags. These Eagles will always serve as rallying points for you; they will go wherever your Emperor deems their presence necessary to defend his throne and his people. You swear to sacrifice your life to

The Army takes an Oath to the Emperor after the Distribution of Eagles, 5 December 1804 by David

defend them,' and many did 'and to maintain them constantly, through your courage, on the road to victory!'

Jacques-Louis David's painting, *The Army takes an Oath to the Emperor after the Distribution of Eagles, 5 December 1804*, now at Versailles, includes a number of notable elements. Napoléon is depicted wearing his *grand habillement*, worn for the Coronation in Notre Dame Cathedral three days previously. Although the 'distribution' was a secular ceremony, unlike the equivalent events in Britain where the Colours are consecrated by the regimental padre before being presented by the Colonel-in-Chief (often, but not always, the sovereign), Napoléon's cumbersome order of dress deliberately gave a quasi-religious significance to the distribution and the soldiers' oath of allegiance. Furthermore, Napoléon's overtly Roman gesture of the raised right arm, known as an *adlocutio*, was used by Roman Generals when addressing their troops. Lastly, although she was present on the day, Joséphine has been excluded from the scene because, by the time the painting was finished in 1810, she had been divorced by the Emperor.

The first recorded capture of an Eagle occurred during the Battle of Austerlitz, when Russian cavalry over-ran the French 4th Infantry Regiment of the Line.* Despite the battle being won by Napoléon, the Eagle was not recovered. Then in 1807, at Battle of Heilsberg, the Eagle of the 55th Infantry Regiment of the

*   The tally of Eagles lost, as recounted here, is neither definitive nor exhaustive.

Line was captured by the Russian Pernov Musketeers, although this is disputed by German military historians, who assert that it was captured by the Prussian Prittwitz Hussars. The same year, the 9th Light Infantry Regiment (The Incomparables) lost their Colour to the Russians at the Battle of Mohrungen; fortunately, the Eagle finial itself, which had fallen off its plinth a few days previously, was in storage awaiting repair. In the same battle, the 27th Light Infantry Regiment briefly lost their Eagle before recovering it. Then, at the Battle of Eylau, the 18th Infantry Regiment of the Line (The Brave) lost its Eagle to the Saint Petersburg Dragoons, which also captured the Eagles of the 16th Light Infantry, the 24th and 44th Infantry Regiment of

Loss of an Eagle at Austerlitz, 2nd December 1805

the Line. The last of these was taken in rather gruesome – but not unusual – circumstances: a cannon ball broke the staff of the 44th's Eagle but, before the Ensign could pick up the finial, a canister round struck him in the chest then a Russian dragoon slashed him across the head. The Saint Petersburg Dragoons must hold the regimental record for captured Eagles. The 24th's replacement Eagle was lost in the Peninsular War (see below) and the 18th lost their second Eagle in 1812 at Krasnoi, when the Regiment was virtually destroyed by the Russian Life Guard Uhlans, during the Retreat from Moscow.

Meanwhile, at the Battle of Bailén in 1808 during the Peninsular War, General Dupont's Corps surrendered to the Spanish and, as part of the capitulation terms, had to give up all of its Colours, including three Eagles belonging to the 1st and 2nd Regiments of the Guard of Paris (not to be confused with the Imperial Guard, who never lost an Eagle) and the 4th Swiss Regiment. These Eagles were kept in Seville Cathedral until they were recovered by the French in 1810 and sent back to Paris. Another Eagle belonging to the 76th Infantry Regiment of the Line was captured by the Spanish at the Battle of Tamames in 1809, but it did not return home and its present whereabouts is unknown.

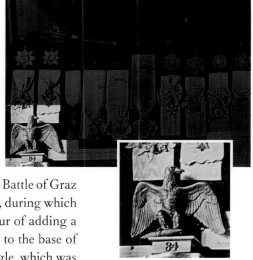

The Eagle of the 84th Infantry Regiment of the Line can be seen in photographs taken in 1905 of the Napoléonic display at the Zeughaus Museum in Berlin. The 84th made their name at the Battle of Graz in 1809, when they fought an heroic action against the Austrians, during which they lost three officers and thirty-one men but gained the honour of adding a brass plaque with the words UN CONTRE DIX ('one against ten') to the base of their Eagle finial. The Regiment later lost their 1804-pattern Eagle, which was destroyed during the Russian Campaign of 1812. At the Battle of Waterloo, they

Eagle of the 84th at the Zeughaus

were part of the 19th Division facing von Bülow's Prussian Corps. Once again heavily outnumbered, they held onto their 1815-model Eagle, only for it to be taken from their depot when the Prussians occupied Paris after the battle.

Far and away the largest number of imperial Eagles were captured by the British, in actions ranging from the West Indies to Waterloo. These are described in detail in *Spoils of War: The Treasures, Trophies and Trivia of the British Army* (Nine Elms Books, 2020), but are summarised here, starting with actions in the French possessions of Martinique and Guadeloupe. These islands were a secure base from which French Navy warships posed a major threat to Britain's trade with its own sugar-producing Caribbean islands. Accordingly, in the autumn of 1808, the British government ordered the Admiralty to send a mixed naval and military force to take out the French threat.

During the successful invasion of Martinique between 30th January and 24th February 1809, the first French regiments to lose their Eagles to the British were the 82nd and 26th Infantry Regiments of the Line, the former's three Eagles being captured by the 7th Regiment of Foot. With Martinique conquered, the British then turned their attention to invading Guadeloupe. On 5th February 1810, the French surrendered. Over 3,500 of their soldiers became prisoners-of-war, and they were forced to give up all their cannons, weapons and the Eagle of the 66th Infantry Regiment of the Line. None of the British regiments involved laid claim to this Eagle, possibly because it had not been captured in action but was handed over under the terms of the French surrender.

Martinique, 21st February 1809

Meanwhile, the British were also fighting the French in Spain and Portugal, under the command of Lieutenant General Sir Arthur Wellesley, the future Duke of Wellington. At the Battle of Talavera in July 1809, the honour of capturing the first French Eagles in the Peninsular War went to the 29th Regiment of Foot. According to the official dispatch, soldiers of the Regiment first seized the Eagle of the French 24th Infantry Regiment of the Line, then wheeled into the flank of the 96th and captured their Eagle as well, although neither was returned to England in what is an enduring mystery. A possible explanation lies in the dispatch, which also records that one of these Eagles was destroyed during the fighting, and the second Colour was without its finial when it was captured.

Two more years were to pass before the next Eagle was captured at the Battle of Barrosa on 5th March 1811. The 87th Regiment of Foot, yelling their fearsome Irish war cry '*Faugh-a-Ballagh*' ('Clear the way') successfully charged the 2nd Battalion of the French 8th Infantry Regiment of the Line and captured their Eagle. The first Irishman to seize the closely guarded Colour was a young officer, Edward Keogh. However, as his hand grasped the staff, he was shot through the heart and then bayoneted. His place was taken by Sergeant Patrick Masterson, who prised the Eagle from the hands of its dying Ensign, and shouted: 'B'jaysus, boys, I have the cuckoo!' He held onto it with Celtic tenacity until the end of the battle.

The Barossa Eagle

Like the Eagle of the 66th, that of the 39th Infantry Regiment of the Line involved no bloody heroics, but was swept away in a river when the French retreated during the Battle of Foz de Arouce on 15th March 1811. Viscount Wellington (as Wellesley had become in 1809) offered a large sum to the Portuguese peasantry for its recovery, which bore fruit in mid-June. However, it is significant that he did not give the Eagle to the 95th Regiment of Foot who had driven the French to a watery grave.

The next Eagles to be captured, from the 22nd and 62nd Infantry Regiments of the Line, were seized at the Battle of Salamanca on 22nd July 1812, although the details of their acquisitions remain in doubt: the 22nd's may have been captured by the 30th Regiment of Foot, and the received wisdom is that the 62nd's was taken by Lieutenant William Pearce of the 2nd Battalion of the 44th (East Essex) Regiment of Foot. Following the defeat of the French at Salamanca, Earl Wellington (his titles rose with his advance through Spain) turned towards Madrid, which was liberated on 12th August 1812. Two Eagles, belonging to the 13th Regiment of Dragoons and the 51st Infantry Regiment of the Line, were found there in storage. The final capture of an Eagle during the Peninsular War happened in July 1813, when that of the 28th Infantry Regiment of the Line was taken in the Maya Pass in the Pyrenees by their British opposite number, the 28th (North Gloucestershire) Regiment of Foot.

Battle of Salamanca, 22nd July 1812

The last two Eagles acquired by the British (both of the 1815 pattern) were seized at the Battle of Waterloo on 18th June 1815. The Scots Greys were part of the Union Brigade deployed against General d'Erlon's Corps, when the latter

Capture of the Eagle of 105th,
Waterloo, 18th June 1815

attacked the left wing of the Anglo-Allied position at around one o'clock. The Greys' charge that followed broke through to the centre of the French infantry as they were forming from column into line. In brisk hand-to-hand fighting, the Eagle of the 45th Infantry Regiment of the Line was seized by Sergeant Charles Ewart.

The story of the capture of the Eagle of the 105th Infantry Regiment of the Line by the 1st (Royal) Regiment of Dragoons (known as The Royals) is less straightforward and still resonates today. That it was also captured during the cavalry charge against d'Erlon's Corps is not in question; it is the identity of the Royal responsible which is still hotly disputed. One version of the story is that Captain Alexander Clark led his Squadron of The Royals around the French flank, caught sight of the Eagle and made to capture it. Later, in a letter to his sister which included some significant inaccuracies about the Eagle, Clark recounted how he ran the French Ensign through the right side above the hip, and then again through the body, but was unable to grab the Eagle, which fell across the horse of Corporal Francis Stiles. Stiles, in a separate account, claimed that Captain Clark had ordered *him* to capture the Eagle. What is not in dispute is that Clark then sent Stiles to the rear with the trophy. So seriously was this dispute taken that an enquiry was ordered by The Royals' Commanding Officer, which lasted until 1816. It would seem that Stiles' account was believed, for he was rewarded for the capture, being made a Sergeant and later an Ensign. However, Clark was having none of Stiles' claims, and over the next twenty-three years he made ten official complaints reasserting his right to be recognised as the man who captured the Eagle of the 105th. The descendants of both men continue to contest their competing claims to the present day.

All of the Eagles captured by the British were, in due course, presented to The Prince Regent, who consigned them to the Chapel Royal. They were moved from there to the Royal Hospital Chelsea in 1835 by the command of King William IV, who had decided to bring together all captured Colours in one place. This decision was reversed after the Second World War when, between 1947 and 1971, the Eagles of 8th, 22nd, 45th, 62nd, 82nd and 105th Infantry Regiments of the Line were presented back to the British regiments that had captured them. The Eagle of the 8th was actually a copy, the original having been stolen in 1852, and only those of the 45th and 105th retained their *drapeaux* by the time they were returned to their captors. Mean-while, the Eagles of 13th, 26th, 39th and the 66th Infantry Regiments of the Line remain at the Royal Hospital while the others are in regimental museums, except for the Eagle of the 105th which is in the National Army Museum, London.

Royal Hospital Handover Parade, 1947

The total number of Napoléonic Eagles captured and not recovered by the French is uncertain but was probably around twenty-five. Thus, somewhat embarrassingly for Napoléon who undoubtedly knew the statistics, nearly as many Eagles were lost by the French in eleven years as were lost by the Romans in four hundred and fifty years. This may be the reason why, after the rout of Joseph Bonaparte's forces in the Peninsular in 1813, the Emperor ordered that all cavalry regiments were to return their Eagles to their home depots, with only the Eagle of the senior cavalry Regiment of each Infantry Brigade (to which it was attached) being allowed to remain in the field.

Of the remaining Eagles – lost, destroyed, or extant but not captured – that of the 86th Infantry Regiment of the Line sank in a storm while returning home to France, after the Convention of Cintra, 1808, which allowed the defeated French to evacuate their troops from Portugal. The Eagle of the 47th Infantry Regiment of the Line was buried during the French retreat from Oporto in 1809, along with three Eagles of the 18th Dragoons. One of the latter reappeared after the Penin-sular War in the hands of a French officer, who had concealed it throughout his time as a prisoner in England and later presented it to Marshal Davout in 1815.

Eagles at the Royal Hospital Chelsea

The number of Eagles in private collections is unknown, although there exist on the web photographs of the Eagles of the 5th, 10th, 25th, 32nd and 143rd Infantry Regiments of the Line none of which are in public collections. A rare naval Eagle sold recently at auction in London for £49,600; and an 1815-pattern Eagle, with no regimental plinth but two bullet wounds and several sword cuts, is in the Bruno Ledoux Collection. For the rest, and excluding those in British military collections, several are held in continental European public collections including

Aigle blessé in Musée
de l'Armée

Aigle blessé formerly in
the Monaco Collection

A Grenadier of the Old Guard

the Eagle of the 6th Regiment of Chasseurs à Cheval, which is owned by the Fondation Napoléon in Paris. An 1804-pattern Eagle, known as the '*aigle blessé*', is in the Musée de L'Armée in Paris, along with two 1815-pattern Eagles, one of which belonged to the 2nd Infantry Regiment of the Line.

Until 2014, there was another 'wounded eagle' in the Prince of Monaco's collection. It was sold at the auction of the museum's contents to a private buyer for a hammer price of €140,000 (£120,000). Both of the '*aigles blessé*' not in the Bernard Ledoux Collection had been shot through with cannister (rather than musket balls), the one in the Monaco collection also having – like the Ledoux example – a number of sabre cuts around the eagle's head, indicating that it had been in the thick of hand-to-hand fighting. To judge from some pre-Second World War photographs of the museum's collection *in situ*, there were actually four Eagles in the Monaco collection, a second one selling at the same auction as the 'wounded eagle' for only €90,000 (£77,000), possibly because it was unscathed. Both of the Monaco Eagles were of the 1804-pattern but, because their regimental numbers are missing, their actual service histories are unknown. That said, the 'wounded eagle' carries the following inscription on the plinth: '*La Garde meurt, mais elle ne se rend pas. 18 Juin 1815.*' ('The Guard dies, but it does not surrender. 18 June 1815.'), by tradition these were the words spoken by General Pierre Cambronne at the Battle of Waterloo when Colonel Hugh Halkett invited the Old Guard of the Imperial Guard to surrender. However, the inscription is probably of a later date and does not necessarily imply that this Eagle belonged to a Regiment of the Imperial Guard. It is also unclear if either of the Monaco collection finials were originally attached to any of the regimental *drapeaux* in the collection. Two of these were sold in 2014, one dating from 1804 and belonging to the IIIth Infantry Regiment of the Line, and the other dating from 1812 and belonging to the 10th Regiment of Cuirassiers. The first sold for €75,000 (£64,000) and the second for €50,000 (£42,750).

Possibly the most valuable of all the seventy-six Eagles believed to have survived the Restoration of the Bourbon monarchy, is the 1815-pattern Eagle finial, *cravat* and *drapeau* of the 1st Regiment of Grenadiers à Pied of the Imperial Guard, the most senior Regiment of Napoléon's Army; interestingly, this 1815 pattern finial has the number '1' on the plinth rather than '*Garde Impériale*' as with the 1804 pattern.

Otherwise known as the Old Guard (*Vielle Garde*) or 'the Immortals', the soldiers who formed the four regiments of infantry (two regiments each of Grenadiers à Pied and Chasseurs à Pied) and five of cavalry (the Grenadiers à Cheval, the Chasseurs à Cheval, the Dragons de l'Impératrice, the 1st Polish Lancers and the Mamelukes) were the elite and veteran element of Napoléon's

Imperial Guard, and provided his personal bodyguard. Better trained and receiving higher rates of pay than the rest of the Imperial Guard and the Army, membership of the Old Guard was restricted to soldiers with a minimum of ten years of service, who had fought in at least three campaigns. The Grenadiers had to be at least 5 feet 10 inches tall and the Chasseurs at least 5 feet 8 inches, and all of them had to have faced enemy fire to the front. In addition to their unique bearskin caps, all members of the Old Guard were granted an imperial dispensation allowing them to air their grievances, as a result of which they were also known as 'the Grumblers'.

Originally in the collection of Count Anatoli Nikolaievich Demidov, Principe di San Donato, the Eagle of the 1st Grenadiers à Pied was not lost in battle. Instead, it probably came into the Russian's possession through his rather unsatisfactory mariage in 1840 to Princesse Matilde-Letizia Bonaparte, the daughter of Napoléon's Jérôme Bonaparte. The Eagle, complete with its well-preserved *cravat* and *drapeau*, was placed on display by the Prince in his fourteen-room museum at the Villa San Donato in Florence, and remained there until the rump of the Demidov collection of artworks was sold in March 1880, ten years after his death.

At this point it was bought for US$300 (1880: £60/2020: £7,500) by the enormously rich American collector, Isabella Stewart Gardner, of Boston, Massachusetts.

below, left to right
Principe di San Donato
(1813–1870); Princesse Matilde-
Letizia Bonaparte (1820–1904);
Isabella Stewart Gardner
(1840–1924) by Sargent

Colour, 1st Regiment of
Grenadiers à Pied of the Imperial
Guard

Eagle finial of 1st Regiment of
Grenadiers à Pied of the Imperial
Guard

Napoléon presents first Legion
of Honour, 16th August 1804,
Boulogne

She placed it on display in 1903 in the Short Gallery of her eponymous mock-Venetian-Renaissance museum in Boston. There it remained until 18th March 1990 when the Eagle finial (but not the *cravat* and *drapeau*) was stolen, along with twelve other unique works of art including Rembrandt's only known seascape. These items were worth an estimated US$500 million in total and the theft, which took just eighty-one minutes, is the largest art heist ever recorded. Despite a reward of US$10 million remaining on offer, none of the works, including the Eagle finial, have ever been recovered.

*   *   *

The second most important Napoléonic prop is the Legion of Honour, which was established by Napoléon during the Consulate in 1802, as an honour for both civilians and soldiers. With later modifications, it has remained in use to the present day. As with so many other things pertaining to the *ancien régime*, the former Christian Orders of Chivalry had been swept away by the French Revolution. In their place, the Consulate created objects 'of honour' to recognise merit. These were originally swords for the military and scarves (*éscharpes*) for civilians. While these were not abolished, they were effectively replaced in 1802 by the establishment of the secular Legion of Honour, which was an Order of Chivalry in all but name.

As before and since, the principal purpose of the new Order was to enable Napoléon to gain or retain loyalty through the award of an honour:

'You call these baubles,' he is recorded as stating, 'well, it is with baubles that men are led ... Do you think that you would be able to make men fight by reasoning? Never. The soldier needs glory, distinctions, rewards.'

As he quickly discovered, once awarded, loyalty could (and sometimes did) evaporate and his original idea of constituting a loyal unit loosely based on the Roman Praetorian Guard, with Legionaries, Officers, Commanders, regional Cohorts and a Grand Council, proved to be for the most part impractical. By the time the Legion of Honour was re-constituted as an imperial institution by a decree on 30th January 1805, it was indistinguishable from its royal predecessors, with ranks and appropriate insignia.

Originally, the highest rank was the Grand Eagle which was designated by a broad red silk riband worn from the right shoulder, a five-pointed silver breast star and other badges, and a heavy gold collar of interlinking imperial eagle which cost F5,000 in 1804 (2020: £13,850). By 1810, Napoléon was depicted wearing a diamond-encrusted Grand Eagle collar with his *petit habillement*, although what it cost and what happened to it after 1815 is unknown. In total, Napoléon awarded fifteen Grand Eagle gold collars to his family and senior officials. The title of Grand Eagle, but not the Legion, was abolished at the Restoration of the monarchy and replaced with a different pattern of collar worn only by the Grand Master, who was head of the Legion after 1815.

The lesser ranks, which have also been amended over the years since 1815, were in descending order: Grand Officer, Commander, Officer and Legionnaire, much in the manner of the ranks within Britain's Orders of Chivalry today. However, in stark contrast to the British, under the French First Empire members of the Legion of Honour were also given a cash grant with a Grand Officer receiving F5,000 (2020: *c.* £13,850) and a Legionnaire receiving F250 (2020: *c.* £692).

Although the records of the Legion were lost in a fire during the Paris Commune of 1871, it is now generally accepted that the stories of three women receiving the Legion of Honour from the Emperor are apocryphal: Virginie Ghesquière certainly served in military drag from 1806-1812 and even rose to the rank of Lieutenant, but there is no hard evidence of her being awarded the Legion of Honour; Marie-Jeanne Schelling was another 'amazon' in uniform who rose to commissioned rank, but the claim that she received the award from Napoléon in June 1808 in Ghent is impossible, as the Emperor is recorded as being elsewhere at the time. Finally, Sister Anne Biget, who selflessly assisted wounded and imprisoned soldiers both before and after the French Revolution, did not receive the Legion of Honour but was awarded the Order of Saint-Michel and the Decoration of the Lily by Louis XVIII. The first woman to be awarded the Legion of Honour was an ancient revoutionary called Lieutenant Marie-Angélique Josèphe Brûlon (née Duchemin). She too had fought in drag in the 1790s, and was admitted as a military pensioner to Les Invalides in 1804. Despite her reputation, and numerous wounds suffered in battle, she only received the decoration in 1851 from Prince-President Louis-Napoléon Bonaparte, who the following year became Emperor Napoleon III.

Despite his initial, revolutionary distaste for chivalric Orders, and his insistence that the Legion of Honour was not one, as Emperor, Napoléon accumulated many foreign Orders and decorations for himself. Most of these were captured after the Battle of Waterloo and are now, as noted in the Introduction, in the State Hermitage Museum collection.

In 1805, he also instituted the royal Italian Order of the Iron Crown with a green-bordered yellow riband. The neck badge consisted of an imperial eagle above a small copy of medieval Iron Crown of Lombardy, which was said to contain a nail from the True Cross and was used for his Coronation in Milan in 1805. The breast badge of the Order was an eight-pointed star with the Emperor's

Napoléon wears the diamond Grand Eagle collar, *c.* 1810

Order of the Iron Crown

classical profile at its centre. There were three ranks: twenty Grand Cross Knights; one hundred Knights Commander; and five hundred Knights. The order was abolished in 1815.

In 1811, Napoléon created the Order of the Reunion, specifically for those serving in France's extended Empire. As with the Order of the Iron Crown, it had three ranks, but unlike the Iron Crown, with its direct reference to the medieval Holy Roman Empire, the regalia of the Order of the Reunion harked back to classical Rome. For on the reverse of a twelve-pointed star, surrounding the letter 'N', was an empty throne in front of which was the instantly recognisable classical Roman motif of the Capitoline Wolf suckling Romulus and Remus. Clearly, even in 1811, Napoléon was careful to maintain the imperial plot line. Like the Order of the Iron Crown, the Order of the Reunion was abolished in 1815.

Order of the Golden Fleece

Finally, in 1809, Napoléon planned a third Order, although this one had no Roman or Holy Roman motif. Nonetheless, the symbology of the Imperial Order of the Three Golden Fleeces contained a clear message. For it was specifically designed to emphasise the Emperor's victory over the Habsburg monarchies of Spain and Austria, both of whom had their own Orders of the Golden Fleece. They were (and still are) highly exclusive decorations that have no direct equivalent in any British Order. As Napoléon stated:

> 'My eagles have triumphed over the Golden Fleeces of the King of Spain and the Emperors of Germany [*sic*], so I mean to create for the French Empire an Imperial Order of the Three Golden Fleeces. The sign of this Order shall be my own Eagle with outspread wings, holding in each of its talons one of the ancient Golden Fleeces it has carried off while, hanging from its beak, it will proudly display the Fleece I now institute.'

The artist Jacques-Louis David's design, much as described above and hanging from a gold-edged red riband beneath which was a cut sapphire mounted between red flames, was approved by Napoléon. The medal-maker Coudray had been selected to make the regalia and a list of first awardees had been drawn up, but the Order was never awarded. Why? Because, in 1810, Napoléon married Marie Louise of Austria and it was no longer politically prudent for him to award an Order that so obviously trumped that of his new father-in-law, Francis II, Emperor of Austria. Thus, the Imperial Order of the Three Golden Fleeces was the prop that never was, which is a pity because it was rather handsome.

Order of the Three Golden Fleeces

* * *

Last but not least of the icons in the imperial props department were the batons of the Marshals of the Empire. As with the previous regime, these batons were covered in blue velvet (on some surviving examples the blue velvet has faded to brown) and capped with gold collars, stamped with the Paris assay and duty marks for the period. Around the top collar in capital letters was the Latin inscription: TERROR BELLI, DECUS PACIS ('terror in war, ornament in peace'). Around the bottom collar, in script, was the Marshal's name and the date of the presentation. All but two of Napoléon's twenty-six Marshals appointed between 1804 and 1815 owned the baton of a Marshal of the Empire, but only nine are now held in public collections.

The first of the two baton-less Marshals was the Polish Prince Józef Ponia-towski, who led two heroic cavalry charges on 10th and 12th October 1813, shortly before the Battle of Leipzig on 17th, actions for which he was promoted to the rank of Marshal. In the withdrawal that followed Napoléon's defeat at that battle, and before his baton could be delivered to him, he was badly wounded

Death of Prince Józef Ponia-towski, 19th October 1813

and drowned in the White Elster river. Rumour had it that his fate was guaranteed by the large money belt that he wore under his tunic: the weight of the gold was so great that he sank like a stone.

The aristocratic Marquis Emmanuel de Grouchy, was more fortunate. Despite being the 2nd Marquess, he had survived the French Revolution, and was appointed a Marshal during The Hundred Days in 1815. However, before he could receive his baton, and because of his lacklustre contribution to the Battle of Waterloo, he was faced with the very real prospect of being court martialled and executed. Fortunately for him, his luck continued to hold and, instead of being shot like Murat and Ney, he was stripped of his (notional) baton and went into exile in the United States. There he remained until 1821, when he was allowed to return to France, albeit without his rank or title. It was only during the reign of King Louis Philippe that he was re-admitted to the Chamber of Peers and again created a Marshal in 1830, albeit of France and not the defunct Empire. Napoléon memorably said: 'Don't give me clever Generals, give me lucky ones'; he would, with hindsight, almost certainly have added that de Grouchy was the exception who proved his rule.

The Marshals' batons on public view in France are those of Davout (although his first baton, lost at Krasnoi in 1812, is in the State Hermitage Museum collection), Jean Lannes, Auguste de Marmont, Jean-Baptiste Bessières, Pierre Augereau, and François Joseph Lefebvre. Auguste de Marmont, created Duc de Raguse in 1808, was, like Davout and de Grouchy, an aristocrat of the *ancien régime*. However, his friendship with Napoléon, forged while they were junior artillery officers, stood him in good stead during the Revolution and afterwards. His record as a General in the field was mixed and he was not one of the first Marshals in 1804, only receiving his baton in 1809. This disappointment may account for his decision to throw in his lot with Louis XVIII in 1814, and to vote

below, left to right
Marshal de Grouchy (1766–1847);
Marshal de Marmont (1774–1852);
Marshal Bessieres (1768–1813);
Marshal Augereau (1757–1816)

in favour of Ney's execution. De Marmont's good fortune did not survive the overthrow of the last Bourbon monarch, King Charles X, and the ascent of his Orleans cousin, King Louis-Philippe, in the July Revolution of 1830. Lucky not to be arrested, he escaped into exile, forfeited his baton and died in Venice. For turning his coat in 1814, de Marmont was execrated in France: the verb '*raguser*', meaning to betray and based on his ducal title, entered the French vocabulary, and children would point him out in the street as 'the man who betrayed Napoléon'. Not a great legacy to accompany his extant baton.

By contrast, the gallant cavalry commander, Jean-Baptiste Bessières, created Duc d'Istrie in 1809, was killed (like Lannes and Duroc) by a ricocheting cannon ball in the opening days of the War of the Sixth Coalition of 1813 to 1814. Although the war led to Napoléon's first abdication, his loyalty to the Emperor was never tested. His baton, along with that of Davout, is in the Musée de l'Armée in Paris.

Pierre Augereau, another of the first Marshals in 1804 and Duc de Castiglione from 1808, initially followed de Marmont's example and threw in his lot with Louis XVIII, but then tried unsuccessfully to go back to Napoléon during The Hundred Days. This indecision earned him the gratitude of neither side. The Emperor charged him with treason in 1815, and he was stripped of his titles and pension by Louis XVIII on his second restoration after the Battle of Waterloo. Augereau died the following year.

François Joseph Lefebvre, a Marshal from 1804 and Duc de Danzig from 1807, followed much the same course as Augereau in 1814. However, in spite of going back to Napoléon in 1815, he kept his rank under Louis XVIII and even had his peerage restored to him in 1819, the year before he died.

Known to be in private collections are the batons of André Masséna, Jean Bernadotte (King Charles XIV John of Sweden and Norway from 1818) and

below, left to right
Marshal Lefebvre (1755–1820);
Marshal Bernadotte (1763–1844);
Marshal Victor (1764–1841);
Marshal Massena (1758–1817)

Marshal MacDonald
(1765–1840)

Marshal Jourdan (1762–1833)
with his baton (see page 97)

Marshal Jourdan's uniform coat

Claude Victor-Perrin's Louis XVIII baton, which was sold to a private collector in the 2014 Monaco sale for €110,000 (£94,000). Victor-Perrin, appointed a Marshal in 1807 and created Duc de Belluno in 1808, had distinguished himself during the Retreat from Moscow. After falling-out with the Emperor in early 1814, he transferred his loyalty, on a permanent basis, to Louis XVIII. This stood him in good stead, earning him a royal baton and further honours and appointments until the July Revolution of 1830 when he retired.

André Masséna, a Marshal from 1804, Duc de Rivoli in 1808 and Prince d'Essling in 1810 was described by the Emperor as 'the greatest name of my military empire'. Despite being sacked by Napoléon in 1811 for defeats during the Peninsular War, his reputation has survived rather better than de Marmont's. This may be because, out of office and in retirement, he did not plot Napoléon's first abdication in 1814 and rallied to his side during The Hundred Days. He was also a member of the court martial that refused to try Ney and, consequently, he did not get a job under Louis XVIII.

In a non-French public collection is the baton awarded to Marshal Étienne MacDonald. However, it is not the one awarded to him by Napoleon in 1809, immediately after the Battle of Aspern-Essling, but is a later one given to him by Louis XVIII. Today it is in the Clan Donald Museum at Armadale Castle on the Isle of Skye. MacDonald, who was the French-born son of a Scotsman from South Uist and Duc de Tarranto from 1809, was ordered by Napoléon to transfer his allegiance to Louis XVIII in 1814. He remained loyal to the King in 1815, and served in high military office until his honourable retirement in 1830.

However, of all the batons of the Marshals of the Empire still on public display, that of Jean-Baptiste Jourdan is the most significant. This is not because of his rather mixed military reputation, but because of what the capture of his baton inspired. Jourdan, like so many of his fellow Marshals, rose from the ranks and thereby proved Napoléon's dictum that every ordinary soldier had a Marshal's baton in his knapsack. However, unlike the other ex-rankers, he owed his more to the patronage of Joseph Bonaparte than he did to his (lack of) skill as a General in the Peninsular War. This may account for why, unlike the other Marshals of the Empire, he was not ennobled by Napoléon.

Although a Marshal's baton did not have the same emotional significance as a regimental Eagle, they were nonetheless highly prized by their owners and were always carried by them when in uniform. It is, therefore, quite surprising that Jourdan left his baton on the battlefield of Vitoria in Spain on 21st June 1813, where it was picked up by Private Paddy Shannon of the 2nd Battalion of the 87th Regiment of Foot, who found it on a pile of abandoned baggage, still in its red-morocco-leather case.

In parenthesis, it is worth mentioning that with the baton was a blue serge uniform jacket that was offered for sale at Mellors & Kirk in September 2018 (Lot 904). Self-evidently that of a General, it almost certainly belonged to Jourdan. The coat sold for £17,000 against a pre-sale estimate of £15,000-20,000.

Back to Jordan's baton, which was in due course passed to General the Marquess of Wellington (as he then was). He in turn forwarded it to the 3rd Earl Bathurst, Secretary of State for War, with a covering letter dated 22nd June 1813, which read in part:

The Prince Regent (1762–1830) and the 1st Duke of Wellington (1769–1852)

'I send this despatch by my ADC Captain Freemantle whom I beg leave to your Lordship's protection. He will have the honour of laying at the feet of HRH The Prince Regent ... Marshal Jourdan's baton of a Marshal of France [*sic*] taken by the 87th Regt.'

The Prince Regent was so delighted with the gift that on 5th July 1813, he wrote back to Wellington:

'You have sent me among the Trophies of your unrivalled Fame, the Baton of a French Marshal and I send you in return that of England. The British Army will hail it with enthusiasm while the whole Universe will acknowledge those valorous Exploits, which have so imperiously called for it ...'

This baton, which was the first ever given to a British Field Marshal, was made of gold, which must have seemed like a very fair exchange to Wellington. It may also account for his diplomatic response to Prinny's self-delusional claim to have led The King's German Legion in a successful charge at the Battle of Waterloo (amongst other unfounded royal claims to military achievements that increased with age). 'I have often heard you Your Majesty say so,' was the Iron Duke's invariable response. The baton makes a gilded connection with Napoléon's props department.

The Duke of Wellington's gold baton

BUILDING AND DRESSING THE SET

'A throne is only a bench covered in velvet'

 o said Napoléon, in what must surely – at a superficial level at least – be one of the most cynically dismissive statements in history, particularly given the extraordinary magnificence of the 'benches' on which he rested the imperial backside from 1804 until 1815. However, as with most Napoléonic pronouncements, a greater truth lies beneath the cynicism: that the trappings of power, and monarchical power in particular, are only a matter of appearance. This was a truth that Napoléon took seriously when it came to the stage upon which he strode, and as with everything else to do with the Emperor, the stage became more magnificent over time.

However, as he hovered in the wings for ten years from 1789, his proposed production was unsure of backers and initially constrained by a lack of money, not to mention the imperatives of a political situation in which thrones and crowns were 'out' and guillotines and Phrygian caps were 'in'. Accordingly, the magnificence of the imperial *mise en scène* had to wait until the curtain rose on the Consulate in 1799, with the classically-themed scenery and props being introduced gradually from then until 1804, when the curtain fell on the first act only to rise on the second, with its set displaying the full panoply of imperial power.

Of course, every production requires a setting in which it can be performed. While normally this would be a building, open air spaces were (as they still are today) also used. The thirteen-year journey to the opening of the imperial 'theatre', however, started in the relatively modest confines of a house at 60 Rue de la Victoire, Paris, in what is now the 9th Arrondissement.

Built in 1776 as 6 Rue Chantereine – the name meant 'singing frogs' and referred to the fact that the area was originally a swamp – the house was leased, on 17th August 1795, by Joséphine, the widowed Vicomtesse de Beauharnais.

Guillotines and Phrygian caps

opposite
Napoléon on his Imperial Throne by Ingres

right
60 Rue de la Victoire
below
Recreation of the veranda
at 60 Rue de la Victoire

Thanks to her successful career between a succession of political bedsheets, since her release from prison the previous year, the future Empress could once again afford a roof over her bed and to have her new house fashionably decorated. With the revolutionary wars raging, the then vogue in interior design reflected the martial spirit of the age. Accordingly, soon after taking possession of the property, Joséphine had installed on the terrace a semi-circular *faux* military tent made of painted wood, lined with striped cotton, and hung with flags and pennants *à la militaire*.

Two months later, Napoléon visited Joséphine at her home for the first time and was impressed with the martial décor on the ground floor, as well as his hostess's skills in the advance to contact, the charge, and the tactical withdrawal in the bedroom above. After their marriage on 9th March 1796, Napoléon took up residence in the Rue Chantereine, although a few days later he left to take command of the Army of Italy. On 28th December 1797, as a tribute to his victories there, the street was renamed Rue de la Victoire and, on 26th March 1798, Napoléon purchased the house. However, the triumphant General only lived in this relatively modest house for two short periods. The first lasted from 5th December 1797, on his return from Italy, to 3rd May 1798, the day he left for Egypt. On his return to Paris from the land of sand on 16th October 1799, he lived in the house for a further month and it was there that the Brumaire Coup was planned.

While he was away in the Levant, in April 1799 Joséphine bought (presumably with Napoléon's money) the significantly larger Château de Malmaison as a retreat away from the heart of Paris. Immediately, and to Napoléon's dismay when he found out, she began an expensive remodelling of the house, in the

Château de Malmaison

newly fashionable style later known as 'First Empire'. At the same time, she created a beautiful garden, famous for its roses and exotic animals. Following her divorce from the Emperor in December 1809, Joséphine remained at the house until her death in 1814, and Napoléon spent his final days in Paris there after abdicating in 1815.

Following the Brumaire coup's successful execution in 1799, as First Consul Napoléon took up residence with Joséphine at the Tuileries Palace in central Paris. Built in the sixteenth-century, with later additions, the palace stood between the Louvre and the Tuileries Garden, leading to the Place de la Concorde, where Louis XVI had been executed in 1793 when it was called the Place de la Révolution. During the French Revolution, the palace was not badly damaged or stripped, as it served both as a venue for successive government assemblies, and a prison for Louis XVI and his family. It even survived being stormed by an armed mob in 1792, who massacred the King's Swiss Guard. Following its

Tuileries Palace on fire, 1871

re-designation as the Paris residence of the First Consul, and from 1804 the imperial palace, it was redecorated in the new style.

After the Restoration of the monarchy, the Tuileries was successively occupied by the Bourbon, Orleans, Second Republic, and Second Empire Heads of State. Napoléon III was the last to live there until his fall in 1870. On 23rd May 1871, during the uprising known as the Paris Commune, the palace was deliberately

destroyed by insurgents using petrol, liquid tar, turpentine and gun powder. The remaining shell was sold in 1882 to an entrepreneur for F33,300 (2020: c. £140,000) and demolished in 1883.

The other principal First Empire residence in Paris was the Élysée Palace. Completed in the French classical style in 1722 for the Comte d'Évreux, after passing through several hands (including those of Louis XV's mistress, Madame de Pompadour), it was acquired by the Duchesse de Bourbon in 1787, then confiscated at the start of the French Revolution and turned into gambling rooms. In 1803 it was acquired by Murat, who sold it to Napoléon in 1808. He designated it as the Paris home of Joséphine following their divorce in 1809. It is ironic that the Emperor spent his last days in Paris in both the homes of his late

below, left to right
Elysée Palace; Palace of Versailles

above, left to right
Petit Trianon, Versailles; Grand Trianon, Versailles

first wife, for it was at the Élysée on 22nd June 1815 that Napoléon signed his second abdication before moving to Malmaison, and eventually to St Helena.

*   *   *

Given that he was out of France for much of his time in power, both as First Consul and then as Emperor, it is at first sight somewhat perplexing that Napoléon should have maintained and occupied quite so many residences outside Paris as he did. The answer is undoubtedly that, as with the establishment of the enormously elaborate Imperial Households, he felt the need to live in as much 'state' as had his royal predecessors, or as befitted his role as the Master of Europe.

Nonetheless, the establishment of the Imperial Court at the Palace of Versailles proved to be impossible because all the furniture, fixtures and fittings of Louis XIV's vast palace had been sold during the Revolution, and the buildings had been turned into a warehouse. The cost of restoring and furnishing the palace's interiors was too great even for Napoléon, who restricted renovation work to the Grand Trianon, which was redecorated and refurnished in the First Empire style for Empress Marie Louise, the Petit Trianon, which underwent the same treatment for his sister, Pauline Borghese, and the former royal stables.

The occupation of other former royal palaces proved to be less costly. Although some were large and had suffered the same fate as Versailles, they were not on such

Château de Saint-Cloud

a grand scale. The first to be restored was the Château de Saint-Cloud, which had come into royal ownership in 1658 when it was bought by the Duc Philippe d'Anjou, the brother of Louis XIV, who became Duc d'Orleans in 1660. Known as 'Monsieur', he had house extensively remodelled and it remained in the Orleans family until Louis XVI bought it for Queen Marie Antoinette in 1785, who carried out further major works. Emptied during the French Revolution, the Orangery at Saint-Cloud was the scene of the Brumaire coup and the declaration of the Consulate. From 1804, the château was Napoléon's principal country residence, but the only building works carried out there were the conversion of the interiors to the First Empire style, and the creation of a throne room. In October 1870, during the closing days of the Franco-Prussian

War, the château was hit by Prussian artillery and destroyed by fire; the remaining shell was demolished in 1891. There is currently discussion in France about rebuilding the château.

In parallel with the redecoration of Saint-Cloud as a country residence, Napoléon gave orders for the restoration of the Château de Fontainebleau, as the principal imperial hunting lodge and the base for the Grand Master of the Imperial Hunt. From the twelfth century onwards, Fontainebleau had been enlarged by successive French Kings as a hunting lodge until Francis I replaced it with a Renaissance château in the sixteenth century. Expansion and embellishments continued until the French Revolution, when all the furniture was sold. Ahead of his Coronation, Napoléon had the château restored, refurnished and, in part, redecorated in the First Empire style. He did not spend much time at Fontainebleau, and between 1812 and 1814 it served as an elegant and comfortable 'prison' for Pope Pius VII. However, it was there in April 1814 that the Emperor signed his first abdication, before attempting suicide with opium, and then bade an emotional farewell to the soldiers of the Old Guard.

The comparatively modest Château de Compiègne had originally been constructed in the fourteenth century as another royal hunting lodge. It was then rebuilt in the mid-eighteenth century for Louis XV, emptied during the French Revolution, and then restored by Napoléon in 1807, predominantly in the First Empire style.

During the Second Empire, it became the autumn residence of the Imperial

Château de Compiègne

Family and some of the rooms were redecorated in the ugly style of that period. Today, the château is a museum where visitors can experience in successive rooms the décor of the *ancien régime*, the First and the Second Empires. The bedrooms of Napoléon I and his two Empresses remain the most impressive.

The story of the Château de Rambouillet is similar to that of Fontainebleau, although the First Empire style modifications were more limited and made later in Napoléon's reign. The remodelling of a second, smaller building on the site commenced in 1784 and was re-named the Palace of the King of Rome following the birth of Napoléon's only son in 1811. Napoléon spent the night of 29th June 1815 at the main château, *en route* to Rochefort and exile on St Helena.

*   *   *

Much has been written about the First Empire style, and a lot of it survives up to the present day, but rather than profile the beautifully crafted furniture, porcelain, silver and other works of art that decorated the imperial palaces, the narrative of this chapter will instead focus on the opening theme before concluding with a look at the Grand Cortège, the Imperial Barge, and the monuments to Napoléon's triumphs that were erected during his reign and which were an important part of the whole imperial production.

Saint-Cloud throne, now at Fontainebleau

*   *   *

Napoléon ordered five imperial thrones from the Parisian workshop of François-Honoré-Georges Jacob-Desmalter. Two were installed in the throne rooms at the Tuileries and Saint-Cloud, although the latter was moved in 1808 to a new throne room at Fontainebleau. One was placed in the Hôtel de Ville in Paris, and the last two were placed in the Senate and Corps Législatif buildings. All these thrones differed from one another in design, although as originally constructed and upholstered, none were over-scale. They generally featured the imperial 'N', laurel leaves, lightning bolts, bees and eagles.

The throne made for Saint-Cloud, still at Fontainebleau, remains in its original state. Interestingly, it features imperial bees rather than an 'N' on the round back and upholstered sides, and has front legs topped with classical busts, ending in lion's paw feet.

The throne made for display in the Tuileries, upholstered in blue velvet like the one now at Fontainebleau, features an 'N' in the centre of the round back and on the side panels; but the arms and legs of the throne are rectilinear in form, and the tops of the front legs are surmounted with medium-sized ivory balls

Tuileries Palace throne

above, left to right
Corps Legislatif throne
(modified); Corps Legislatif
throne (original); Senate throne;
Hôtel de Ville throne

decorated with inset gold lozenges. This Napoléonic 'bench' is now on display in the Louvre Museum. With some minor artistic variations, it is the one depicted in the portrait of the Emperor by François Gérard, *Napoleon I in his Coronation Robes*, that hangs at Versailles.

The throne installed in the Corps Legislatif building is now in the Musée des Arts Décoratifs in Paris. It is covered in heavily embroidered red velvet and is more Renaissance than First Empire in design. As depicted in a painting by Isabey, now in the Kunsthistoriches Museum in Vienna, this velvet-covered bench originally featured imperial eagles either side of the backrest; but it was extensively remodelled after 1815, when most of the imperial symbology was removed, the eagles were replaced with pine cones, and the back surmounted by a gilt crown.

The throne made for the Senate building, also designed more in the style of the Renaissance than the First Empire, remains on display there, although not in its original place. Upholstered in red velvet, it features arms and front legs fashioned to look like winged sphinxes, and has an 'N' embroidered on the straight-topped back, framed by bees in linked cartouches.

The imperial thrones made for the Hôtel de Ville is now in the Ledoux Collection. Once again upholstered in red velvet and featuring the imperial 'N', it shares the First Empire-style rounded backs of the Saint-Cloud and Tuileries models, but has front legs resting on lion's paws with the arms supported by female herms.

Interestingly, none of the five authenticated thrones look exactly like the one depicted in the famous painting, *Napoléon I on his Imperial Throne* by Jean-Auguste-Dominique Ingres, which is now in the Musée de l'Armée. Probably using artistic licence to create the maximum imperial effect, this blue-velvet-upholstered throne is distinctly over-scale and features front legs in the form of Corinthian columns, topped with large, solid ivory balls.

above, left to right
The sixth throne; chair at
Royal Palace of Caserta

Somewhat intriguingly, a possible sixth imperial 'throne' was offered for sale in 2018 by Christie's in New York. Their auction catalogue stated that it was a late-nineteenth century copy, and it sold for US$6,875 (c. £5,300). The same chair, but with a new swab cushion, was offered the following year by the French auctioneer, Osenat. Upholstered in red velvet and featuring the iconic 'N' on the rounded back, it is similar in design to the Tuileries model, but less elaborate. It was de-accessioned and placed in the Christie's sale by the San Francisco Museum of Fine Arts, which had owned it for more than a century. When it came up for sale at Osenat its authenticity was challenged by Bruno Ledoux of the eponymous Collection. He stated on French television that it was a 'bad copy'.

Two alternative explanations exist: first, that this 'throne' was originally installed at Saint-Cloud and, contrary to accepted belief, remained there, with the blue velvet one at Fontainebleau being specially commissioned for that chateau, although there is apparently no documentary evidence of this; second, and a more probable explanation, is that it is not a throne at all but a 'presentation armchair' of the type made by Jacob-Desmalter for, amongst other settings, the Emperor's Grand Cabinet in the Tuileries, an example of which is now in the Royal Palace of Caserta in Italy.

Whatever the truth of the matter, even with Christie's and Ledoux's opinion and without a fully documented provenance, the 'sixth throne' sold in the Osenat sale for £430,000 against a pre-sale low estimate of just over a tenth of that figure, thereby proving the truth (or otherwise) of the Emperor's aphorism.

*   *   *

Napoléon and Marie Louise
Wedding Grand Cortège,
2nd April 1810, Paris

Less contentious than the 'sixth throne' are the various remnants in public collections of the Grand Cortège, the name given to the grand carriage processions of the Emperor and his Court that were assembled for State occasions and were organised by the Grand Equerry. The two most lavish of these events were the Coronation Grand Cortège of 1804 and the Wedding Grand Cortège of 1810, both of which presented the Grand Equerry and his department with considerable challenges.

For the Coronation procession in 1804, the difficulties arose because the old royal stables at Versailles had been abandoned during the Revolution, when the horses, harnesses and saddlery were sold, and the carriages either destroyed or repurposed. In 1810, but not in time for his marriage procession, Napoléon gave orders that the former royal stables at Versailles be completely restored and re-equipped. However, this work was not completed until 1812, prior to which the imperial stables were split principally between the Hôtel de Longueville, near the Tuileries in Paris, and a former Ursuline convent near Saint-Cloud.

In 1804, the newly-appointed Grand Equerry, Marquis Armand-Augustin-Louis de Caulaincourt, was given the largest budget of all the departments in the Imperial Household. He was also given just three months to assemble 152 carriage horses and twenty-five coaches from scratch for the Coronation Grand Cortège. This task, which cost F380,000 (2020: £1,052,600) in addition to the departmental budget, included the construction of a new imperial coach, to be drawn by eight dun-coloured Andalusian horses. The carriage was covered in gold leaf and surmounted by the imperial crown supported by four gilded eagles.

Six years later, the imperial hubris was such that, with just *one* month's notice and an additional budget of F556,983 (2020: £1,542,851), the Grand Equerry's department was commanded to create a Wedding Grand Cortège of 244 carriage horses and forty gala coaches. This was fifteen carriages more than in 1804, ten more than had ever been assembled for ceremonial processions during the *ancien régime*, and thirty-four more than were fit-for-purpose in the Imperial Mews at that date.

General de Nansouty (1768–1815)

In the absence of de Caulaincourt, who was serving as the French Ambassador in Saint Petersburg, his deputy the First Equerry, General Comte Étienne-Marie-Antione de Nansouty, immediately ordered the refurbishment of the six existing gala carriages, including the imperial coach used at the Coronation. He also placed orders with thirteen Parisian coachbuilders for thirty-two new gala coaches, and ordered two lavish six-seater carriages for the Emperor and the Empress from Getting. The imperial couple travelled in the refurbished Coronation coach, immediately behind the new coach made for the Empress, which was drawn by eight grey horses and designated the *Chariot du Corps*. By royal and now imperial tradition, the *Chariot du Corps* always travelled empty, although in that role it was accorded 'full honours'.

As if the imperial command for the Marriage Grand Cortège was not enough with which to be contending, the First Equerry had the additional problem that Napoléon took a close interest in the build of the new coaches, worried that – despite the huge budget allocated – the speed of construction would result in shoddy workmanship. He need not have been concerned because, thanks to the meticulous supervision

General Daru (1767–1829)

Mameluke
of the Imperial Guard

of their construction by the Intendant General, Comte Pierre-Antoine-Noël-Bruno Daru, these new vehicles passed their final quality inspection, albeit only two days before the ceremony.

The Emperor's purpose in ordering such a lavish Wedding Grand Cortège was, of course, to create a spectacle worthy of his new royal bride, while at the same time setting a new standard of State ceremonial befitting his self-appointed role as the Master of Europe. This latest grand imperial display was nearly destroyed by heavy rain that fell during the twenty-four hours preceding the big day. Fortunately for all concerned, particularly the First Equerry, the clouds vanished on the morning of 2nd April 1810 as the Wedding Grand Cortège set off from Saint-Cloud and headed for the Louvre's Salon Carré, where the religious wedding ceremony was to be held.

The route from Saint-Cloud to the altar entered Paris at the Porte Maillot, and continued to the part-constructed Arc de Triomphe at the Place de l'Étoile, where the procession stopped for the Emperor to receive civic addresses. It then travelled down the Champs-Élysées to the Tuileries and the Louvre. From the entrance to Paris, the processional way was lined by huge crowds, who were held back by infantry units of the Imperial Guard.

As with all such parades in France and elsewhere, both before and since, the magnificence of the carriage procession was considerably enhanced by its mounted escort. Leading the Cortège, taking post between the carriages that followed, and tail-ending the procession, were divisions of the extravagantly uniformed Grenadiers à Cheval, Chasseurs à Cheval, Dragons de l'Impératrice, 1st Polish Lancers and the exotically-dressed Mamelukes of the Imperial Guard.

The first carriage in this huge convoy was occupied by the assistants to the Grand Master of Ceremonies; the next nine conveyed the Chamberlains of the Empire and the Kingdom of Italy; these were followed by four coaches containing the Grand Officers of the Empire and a further four with government Ministers; behind these were eight carriages for the Ladies-in-Waiting of France and Italy, and the Grand Officers of the Crown of Italy; next in the Cortège were the Grand Master of Ceremonies and the Grand Chamberlain together in a single coach, followed by four coaches containing the Imperial Princes and Princesses. Next came the *Chariot du Corps*, followed by the Coronation coach in which sat Napoléon and Marie Louise. The imperial conveyance was escorted by young pages *à pied* and the prancing horses of the Marshals of the Empire, the First Equerry (in place of the Grand Equerry), the Grand Equerry of the Kingdom of Italy and the First Equerry to the Empress. Behind the imperial pair's gilded coach and its escort was the Emperor's new carriage containing the Grand Chaplain, the Grand Marshal of the Palace, and the Grand Master of the Hunt. The last of

the carriages in the Cortège contained the Ladies of Honour and lesser members of the Imperial Family, followed by yet more divisions of the Garde à Cheval.

It must have been every bit as magnificent a procession as the Emperor had intended, and was described by an aristocratic eyewitness with these words:

above, left to right
Grenadiers à Cheval and Chasseurs à Cheval of the Imperial Guard

> '...the brilliant *equipages*, one after the other in such great numbers, the richness and variety of the clothes, the beauty of the women, the brilliance of the diamonds, everything was spectacular...it is difficult to give an accurate picture of such splendour.'

Very few of the carriages from this Grand Cortège remain, although items of harness and some of their fixtures and fittings occasionally find their way onto the open market, sometimes being acquired by public collections. Fortunately, the carriage known as *Victory*, used at Napoléon's Coronation, survives at Versailles. However, like its Bourbon predecessor which was deliberately destroyed

The Imperial Barge

during the Revolution, the Coronation coach itself was demolished on the orders of Louis XVIII at the Restoration of the monarchy.

This was not a fate that befell the Imperial Barge, built in 1810 in just three weeks: speed was ever the Napoléonic Order of the Day, be it on land or sea. It was created to convey the Emperor and his new Empress on a grand water-borne inspection of new warships being constructed for the French Navy in the dockyards of Antwerp. Sixty feet long, the barge, which was recently restored, was crewed by twenty-two oarsmen, each manning a single oar on the port and starboard sides. At the stern is a large cabin with a domed roof, surmounted by a large imperial crown carried by *putti*, and at each of the corners are martial helmets. The prow was originally decorated with a large, gilded imperial eagle, but in 1858 the Emperor's nephew, Napoleon III, had it removed and replaced with a triton-wielding figure of Neptune astride a dolphin and supported by *putti*. It is an impressive sight.

Nevertheless, there are no records of Napoléon using the barge again. After a brief return to favour during the Second Empire, it was left in Brest where it remained until 1943 when, to protect it from Allied bombing raids on the port, it was moved to the Musée National de la Marine at the Palais Chaillot in Paris. Too large to fit through the museum's entrance, it was left outside at the mercy of the weather for two years, until a large hole was made in the wall of the building, and it was finally installed in 1945. In 2018, following a £1,000,000 restoration project, it was returned to Brest and given a place of honour within the town's Musée de la Marine.

* * *

Although during the First Empire the imperial barge never sailed past monuments to the Imperial Impresario, other than a nascent fleet that never saw action, it was altogether a different matter for the Wedding Grand Cortège, which (as already noted) paused at the Arc de Triomphe de l'Étoile. This grand monument, visible from much of central Paris, was commissioned by Napoléon in 1806 to commemorate his victories in Europe, and to honour soldiers who had fought and died in the French Revolutionary and Napoléonic Wars. It was designed by Jean Chalgrin, who based it on the Arch of Titus in Rome. It took two years just to lay the foundations, and a wooden mock-up had to be erected around the building works for the Wedding Grand Cortège. Given its status today as one of Paris's most famous icons, it is worth recording that construction was halted after Napoléon's abdication in 1814, and only recommenced in 1833 on the orders of King Louis Phillipe, with completion three years later.

Having travelled on down the Champs-Élysée from the Place de l'Étoile, the next Napoléonic monument on the route of the matrimonial convoy was the Arc de Triomphe du Carrousel. This altogether smaller edifice was based on the triumphal arches of the Roman Empire, particularly the Arch of Constantine, and was erected to commemorate, *inter alia*, Napoléon's victory the Battle of Austerlitz in 1805. It was designed by Charles Percier and Pierre François Léonard Fontaine, and erected between 1806 and 1808 as the main gateway to the Tuileries Palace. It was surmounted by a quadriga which, during the First Empire, consisted of the Horses of Saint Mark's Basilica in Venice, looted by Napoléon in 1797 but returned to that city in 1815 on the orders of his father-in-law, Francis I of Austria.

The Wedding Grand Cortège came to a final halt at the Louvre, which had originally been built in the twelfth century as a royal palace and extended many times by later monarchs. In 1793, a year after the execution of Louis XVI, it was repurposed as a national museum. Under Napoléon, a north wing was commenced and the museum became the repository for Frances's spoils of war. In 1803, the entire museum was re-named the Musée Napoléon but the original name was restored 1815, and some (but not all) of the looted artworks were returned to their countries of origin.

Not on the route of either the Coronation or the Wedding Grand Cortèges were further neo-classical monuments erected during the First Empire. These included the Fontaine du Palmier in the Place du Châtelet, one of fifteen fresh-water drinking fountains in Paris, commissioned by Napoléon in 1806. The

below, left to right
Fontaine du Palmier, Place du Châtelet, Paris; Arc de Triomphe du Carrousel, Paris

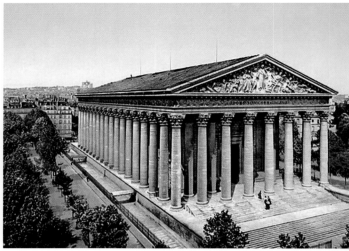

above, left to right
Vendôme Column in the Place
Vendôme, Paris, *c.* 1900;
L'église de la Madeleine, Paris

design, by the engineer François-Jean Bralle, derived from a Roman triumphal column and celebrated, in particular, Napoléon's Egyptian Campaign of 1798 to 1801; it was completed in 1808.

A more important columnar monument, and one with a more chequered history, is the Vendôme Column in the Place Vendôme. Erected to celebrate the Battle of Austerlitz in 1805, the original design of 1806 was based on that of Trajan's Column in Rome. Clad in bronze *bas reliefs* depicting Napoléonic battle scenes, cast from captured Russian and Austrian cannons, the column was originally topped by a bronze statue of Napoléon in Roman robes. After the Restoration of the monarchy in 1814, the statue was destroyed on the order of the Allies, although the iron model from which it was cast survived and was sold at Bullock's 1819 auction (Lot 105 on the first day of the sale) to a Mr Hume for £32.12.0 (2020: £3,028), just £2.12.0 (2020: £242) more than its scrap value. According to the catalogue, Bullock had obtained the two-ton model from the 'Museum of Antiquities', but where that was located or when it was acquired is not explained in the notes to the Lot. The plinth at the top of the column remained vacant until 1831, when a replacement statue of Napoléon in his iconic uniform and bicorne hat was installed. This in turn was replaced by Emperor Napoléon III in 1863 with a statue of his uncle, once more in classical attire. The entire column was dismantled during the Paris Commune of 1871, although the *bas reliefs* were preserved, and it was re-erected in 1873–75 with a copy of the original statue once more at the apex.

A short walk away from the Vendôme Column in L'église de la Madeleine. The imperial origin of this church dates from 1806, when Napoléon decided to

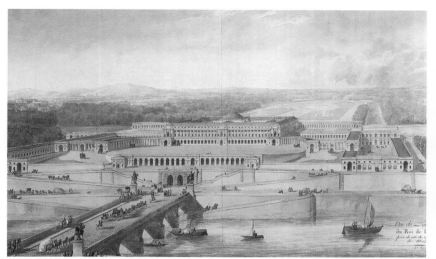

above, left to right
Proposed Palace of the King of
Rome, Paris; Rue de Rivoli, Paris

erect a secular *Temple de la Gloire de la Grande Armée*, on the site of a part-constructed church and using the already-constructed columned portico. The design by Pierre-Alexandre Vignon was based on the Maison Carrée, a well-preserved Roman temple in Nîmes. The building was incomplete at the time of the fall of the First Empire in 1814, the nave was eventually roofed in 1831, and it was considered for use as a railway terminus in 1837. It was finally consecrated as a Catholic church in 1842. Napoléon commissioned another Roman temple-style building to house the Paris Stock Exchange. Known as the Palais Brongniart, work commenced in 1808, but it was not completed until 1826.

The last of Napoléon's changes to central Paris to be considered here, but the first to be built, was the Rue de Rivoli, construction of which commenced in 1804 to commemorate the Battle of Rivoli of 1797. As anyone visiting Paris today will know, it is a very practical monument in the form of a neo-classical, arcaded street running along the northern side of the Louvre to the Tuileries Garden.

Had he reigned for longer, it is certain that Napoléon would have continued to re-model Paris and to erect further monuments to his triumphs. One such plan, which never left the drawing board, was to build a vast neo-classical Parisian palace for his son, the King of Rome. Designed by Pierre François Leonard Fontaine, it was to stand at the centre of a new imperial government quarter on the site of what is now the museum complex known as the Palais de Chaillot. Neither it, nor the new quarter, were commenced before the First Empire finally ended in 1815.

ON TOUR

'An army marches on its stomach'

APOLÉON'S GREATEST contribution to the art of warfare can be summed up in the word 'speed'. Before his arrival on the global stage, armies lumbered from one contest to another, moving not at the pace of a marching soldier, but at that of the slowest baggage waggon. A vast fleet of these vehicles travelled behind the armies of the day, carrying everything from food, equipment and ammunition, to loot, booty and the soldiers' night time companions, some of whom were their wives but who were, nonetheless, shared out as required.

As Alexander Frater describes in *Chasing the Monsoon*:

'A typical Captain went into battle [in late-eighteenth-century India] with a large bed, several chairs, a folding table, two pairs of candle shades, twenty-four linen suits, several dozen bottles of wine, brandy and gin, a hamper of live poultry, a milch goat, seven trunks containing cooking utensils, cutlery, crystal and table linen, and a palanquin [a covered litter carried by four bearers].'

With the exception of the palanquin, it was the same in Europe.

However, while the range of impedimenta that accompanied Napoléon on campaign was not very different to that described by Frater, there was less of it and it was so arranged that the baggage waggons travelled at the same pace as a marching soldier, not the other way around. It was for these reasons that he was able to move the 180,000-strong Grande Armée from Boulogne to the banks of the Rhine in 1805, a distance of some 400 miles, in just under three weeks, covering an average of twenty miles a day. In the age before mechanisation, that was an unheard-of feat and it took the Austrian Army completely by surprise.

opposite
Napoleon Crossing the Alps
by Paul Delaroche, 1850

En route to Ulm, 1805

While the comfort of the Emperor's ordinary soldiers and officers was to some extent compromised on the altar of speed, Napoléon and his Marshals managed to maintain a high standard-of-living in the field. This was particularly true of the Emperor himself. His transport was the responsibility of the Grand Equerry and his department, just one of the various teams within the Imperial Household employed to create the 'greatest show on earth'. Although the Grand Equerry's responsibilities encompassed everything from the Emperor's ceremonial to his private travel, both of which were done in considerable style as described earlier, this chapter focusses on Napoléon's mobile office-and-home-away-from-home arrangements – and two purpose-built carriages in particular.

During his reign, the Emperor spent more time abroad than he did in France. It was, therefore, for him to be able to maintain his administrative grip wherever he happened to be, without sacrificing his high standards of comfort and personal cleanliness. To achieve this required a considerable wheeled infrastructure. During the Russian Campaign of 1812, Napoléon's personal convoy consisted of fifty vehicles, five hundred horses and six hundred men. Using this wheeled infrastructure, his personal staff were able to set up every aspect of the Emperor's mobile palace in a matter of minutes, whether in a soggy field or in a commandeered castle.

Behind this efficiency lay the application of clever design and engineering to every component of the convoy, from the folding pavilion-tent and the collapsible bed ingeniously stored on a specially designed vehicle, to the extraordinary kitchen on wheels (*La Cuisine Roulante*) that is now on display at Les Invalides in Paris. The details of the Emperor's travelling arrangements were, in fact, so extensive that they have given rise to several books. Accordingly, this chapter focusses further on the arrangements made for Napoléon during The Hundred Days – and it also addresses the myths connected with the capture of his personal carriages in the immediate aftermath of Waterloo.

To set this in context, by the time the Emperor left Paris on 12th June 1815 to face Wellington and Blücher at Waterloo, his personal wheeled infrastructure had – for reasons of speed and economy – been reduced from the fifty carriages and waggons of the Imperial Convoy that set off for Moscow, to three much smaller groups.

In the first group were six vehicles carrying Napoléon's wardrobe, linen, food, stores, furniture and other equipment (including the imperial tent) required for his daily routine of work, eating, bathing and sleeping. This was

Grand Equerry de Caulaincourt

followed, at an interval allowing sufficient time for the first group to do their set-up work, by the second element of the convoy. In these carriages travelled his personal office staff, with all their equipment from maps to ink. Allowing enough time for Napoléon's personal to unpack their desks, the third part of the convoy then departed. This consisted of the Emperor's own travelling coach, a *landau* known in the Imperial Household as *La Dormeuse* ('The Sleeper'), which he shared on the move (but not at night) with his Chief of Staff, Marshal Berthier. A second coach, a *berline*, carried his ADCs and a *bastardelle*, which was a closed, lightweight carriage, was occupied by his personal secretary. The three carriages were escorted by Chasseurs à Cheval of the Imperial Guard.

La Cuisine Roulante

La Dormeuse had been ordered for Napoléon by Empress Marie Louise in 1812, at a cost of F34,000 (2020: *c.* £94,180) from Jean Simons of Brussels and Paris. Simons was a *nouveau riche* coachmaker, who had prospered during the French Revolution and whose Paris workshop had earlier built Napoléon's French Coronation coach. The coachmaker had acquired that contract when by his singer-actress wife, Amélie-Julie Candeillé, introduced him to the Empress Joséphine. This doubtless cost Simons a hefty commission to the then Empress.

However, *La Dormeuse* was constructed not in Paris, but in the unfashionable Rue de la Blanchisserie in Brussels. These workshops were immediately adjacent to a house which Simons had been obliged to acquire because of a lack of property in the more fashionable centre of the city. In 1814, and safely out of harm's way in Paris, Simons let his property in Brussels to General the Duke of Richmond and Lennox, who – as the present Duke explains in the Foreword – initially took the house as part of an economy drive. However, in 1815 the property at 23 Rue de la Blanchisserie also provided the Duke with a base for his command of Wellington's reserve troops in the city, and allowed him to be near his son and heir, Charles Lennox, Earl of March, who, having been badly wounded in the closing stages of the Peninsular War the previous year, was then serving as ADC to the Prince of Orange. With unintentional historic irony, the Duchess of Richmond used the showroom of the empty coachworks, where *La Dormeuse* had been made, as the setting for her ball on Thursday 15th June 1815, three days before the Battle of Waterloo. The Duchess's party was rated by the noted historian, Elizabeth Longford, as 'the most famous ball in history'.

Napoléon's campaign tent and furniture

Back to the carriages: Napoléon had a second *dormeuse*, made by Getting of Paris at a cost of F10,282 (2020: *c.* £28,481), but it was not available during The Hundred Days. In any event, it was Simons' *La Dormeuse*, drawn by six brown Normandy-bred horses, with two postillions and driven by the Emperor's personal coachman, Jean Hornn (a Belgian born in Bergen-op-Zoom in 1788), that had carried the Emperor from Paris to Moscow and back. During the retreat

La Dormeuse

The Duchess of Richmond's
Ball, 15th June 1815

in the snow, the carriage's wheels were removed and it was strapped onto a sled.
It had also accompanied Napoléon to exile in Elba in 1814 (without Hornn), and
returned with him to France in 1815 for The Hundred Days.

Given the fate of this carriage and its contents after Waterloo, it is worth
quoting a contemporary description of it, written shortly after the battle and
reproduced in Bullock's 1819 auction catalogue:

'The exterior of the carriage is, in many respects, very like the modern English
travelling chariots. The colour is a dark blue, with a handsome border ornamented in
gold... the Imperial arms are emblazoned on the bullet proof pannels [sic] of the
doors. It has a lamp at each corner of the roof, and there is one lamp fixed at the back
which can throw a strong light into the interior.

In the front there is a great projection; the utility of which is very considerable.
Beyond this projection, and nearer to the horses, is a seat for the coachman: this is
ingeniously contrived, so as to prevent the driver from viewing the interior of the

carriage; and it is also placed so as to afford those within, a clear sight of the horses, and of the surrounding country…

The pannels [*sic*] of the carriage are bullet proof; at the hinder part is a projecting sword case, and the pannel [*sic*] at the lower part of the back is so contrived, that it may be let down, and therefore facilitate the addition or removal of conveniences [chamber pots], without disturbing the traveller.

The under-carriage, which has swan-neck iron cranes, is of prodigious strength; the springs are semi-circular, and each of them seems capable of bearing half a ton; the wheels, and more particularly the [iron] tires, are also of very great strength. The pole is contrived to act as a lever, by which the carriage is kept on a level on every kind of road. The undercarriage and wheels are painted in vermillion, edged with the colour of the body, and heightened with gold. The harness… bears strong marks of its service in the Russian Campaign and is [recognisable as Imperial equipage] only by the bees, arms and eagles, which are to be seen in several places.

The interior . . . is adapted to the various purposes of an office, a bed-room, a dressing-room, a kitchen, and an eating-room.

The seat has a separation [to prevent the Emperor and Berthier being thrown together by a jolt] . . . In front of the seat are compartments for every utensile [*sic*] of probable utility; of some there are two sets, one of gold and the other of silver. Among the gold articles are a teapot, a coffee pot, sugar basin, cream ewer, coffee cup and saucer, slop basin, candlesticks, wash-hand basin, plates for breakfast etc. Each article is superbly embossed with the imperial arms, and engraved with an 'N'. By the aid of a lamp, anything could be heated in the carriage.

Beneath the coachman's seat is a small box about two and a half feet long, and about four inches square: this contains a [folding] bedstead of polished steel, which could be fitted-up within one or two minutes. The carriage also contains mattresses and other requisites for bedding, of very exquisite quality; all of them commodiously arranged. There are also articles for strict personal convenience [chamber pots] made of solid silver, with silver gilt interiors, fitted into the carriage [below the passenger seat].

A small mahogany case, about ten inches square by eighteen inches long, contains the peculiar *nécessaire de voyage* of the ex-Emperor. It is somewhat in appearance like an English writing desk [slope?], having the imperial arms most beautifully engraved on the cover. It contains nearly one hundred articles, almost all of them in solid gold.

The liquor case, like the *necessaire*, is made of mahogany: it contains two bottles; one [containing] rum, the other some fine old Malaga wine. Various articles of perfumery are among the luxuries which remain [including] Windsor soap, and some English court-plaster, eau de Cologne, eau de Cavande, salt spirit etc.

There is a writing desk, which may be drawn out so as to write while the carriage is proceeding; an inkstand, pens, etc were found in it … and the Emperor's portfolio.

Napoléon's *berline*

In the front there also many small compartments, for maps and telescopes; on the ceiling of the carriage is a net for carrying small travelling requisites.

On one of the doors of the carriage are two pistol holsters, in which were pistols manufactured at Versailles; and in the holster, close to the seat, a double-barrelled pistol also was found . . . all were loaded. On the side there hung a large silver chronometer with a silver chain . . . by Mugnier of Paris.

The doors of the carriage have locks and bolts: the blinds, behind the windows, shut and open by means of a spring, and may be closed so as to form an almost impenetrable barrier.

On the outside of the window[s] [are] roller blind[s] made of strong painted canvas: when pulled down [they prevent rain, snow and damp] from penetrating.'

The second carriage in the third part of the Emperor's convoy has often been promoted by many authorities, most of whom should know better, as Napoléon's principal campaign carriage. It was not. This smaller and less well-equipped carriage, a *berline*, still exists and can be viewed at Malmaison. It was made by Getting in 1812, specifically – like *La Dormeuse* – for the Russian Campaign. Instead of a fixed top, it had two folding roofs, fore and aft, that allowed it to be used in fine weather as an open-topped carriage. To put these vehicles into a modern context, today *La Dormeuse* would be a Winnebago, parked up for the duration of a holiday, and the *berline* would be the small 'runabout' car used by the family to make short trips to the supermarket and the beach.

Meanwhile, back in Belgium ... as the light started to fail at Waterloo at 8pm on Sunday 18th June 1815, the only French soldiers still holding their ground around the Emperor's command post, near the inn known as La Belle Alliance, were the two regiments of the Grenadiers à Pied of the Old Guard formed-up in squares. Their job was to guard Napoléon, who commanded the unit on the left of the inn, and who had by that time realised that the day was lost and that his place was in Paris.

With his iconic charger, *Marengo*, lying wounded in a ditch on the battlefield, Napoléon withdrew from the affray on a spare horse. Escorted by the Chasseurs à Cheval, he made his way to a farm house called Le Caillou, between La Belle Alliance and Genappe, where he had spent the previous night and where the three coaches of the third element of his personal convoy awaited him. Once there, he clambered aboard *La Dormeuse*, and accompanied by the Chasseurs à Cheval and the Getting-made *berline*, Napoléon's campaign coach then trundled off in the direction of Genappe, hotly pursued by Prussian light infantrymen, lancers and British cavalry.

The Old Guard at Waterloo, 18th June 1815

At around 11pm the remains of the imperial convoy had to make a detour through a field just north of Genappe, in order to get around the village which was blocked with fleeing Frenchman. What happened next is recounted in an affidavit, sworn by Hornn in London in 1816 before the Lord Mayor. As a first-hand, sworn account, it is more reliable than others, which differ in substance and detail. It is possible, but perhaps understandably not mentioned in the affidavit, that by going 'off road' the carriage became stuck in the water-logged ground and that is why it was overtaken by the Prussians. It had been raining heavily the previous night and that morning.

For whatever reason, the off-road detour around Genappe allowed the Prussians, led by Major Freiherr (Baron) Heinrich Eugen von Keller of the Prussian 15th Infantry Regiment of the Line, to catch up with the coaches. As can be seen in a contemporary engraving of the scene, von Keller's fusiliers immobilised Napoléon's escape vehicle by bayonetting *La Dormeuse*'s two lead horses and their postillion, while the Baron hacked at Hornn the coachman, before moving to the offside door to seize the occupant of the coach. Hornn later recorded that he was left for dead by the side of the road, stripped of his clothes by Belgian scavengers, and then rescued six days later by a British officer, who took him to Brussels where his wounds were dressed and his right arm was amputated.

The incident at Genappe,
11pm on 18th June 1815

THE CAPTURE of the N

OF BONA

TAKEN ON THE NIGHT OF T

and now exhibiting by pe

at

London Muse

'He leaped out & jumped upon his Horse wi

LITARY CARRIAGE

ARTE

BATTLE OF WATERLOO

sion of Government

Piccadilly.

his Sword, losing his Hat which fell off
(vide Bluchers Letter,)

Published as the Act directs 1st. Jan.y 1816. by W. Bullock London Museum Piccadilly

Napoléon's pocket book

Meanwhile, in the time that it had taken the Prussian officer to inflict ten sword cuts on the unfortunate Hornn, Napoléon had jumped out through the nearside door of *La Dormeuse*. Such was his haste, that his hat fell off and he had no time to put on his greatcoat and sword, but mounted one of his escort's chargers and, 'with tears streaming down his face', continued his headlong flight back to Paris leaving the *landau* and the *berline* stuck in the mud.

In accordance with 'the usage and practice of war', von Keller claimed both carriages and their contents as 'spoils of war', and therefore his property, before leading his men off south to Millet. There they captured the baggage train of the French Army of the North, three thousand Frenchmen (including many senior officers), eighty cannon and a huge stash of diamonds hidden in gunpowder kegs. For this action, and the capture of Napoléon's carriages, von Keller was awarded the prestigious Prussian decoration, *Pour le Mérite*.

While von Keller was busy in Millet, a Troop of the British 15th Hussars came across Napoléon's abandoned carriages. Corporal Henry Rolfe of the 15th leaned from his saddle, and through one of the open windows of *La Dormeuse* grabbed what he described as the Emperor's 'grey cloak', in an inside pocket of which he found a pocketbook embroidered with beads and lined with green silk. The 'grey cloak' was in fact Napoléon's greatcoat (cavalry greatcoats are known as 'cloaks', despite having sleeves), which had been abandoned in the carriage when the Emperor escaped from the Prussians.

Rolfe told no one what he had taken and retained the pocketbook until his death, when it passed to his wife. She in turn gave it to a friend, who

Napoléon's greatcoat clasp

passed it on to Captain James Gordon of the 15th Hussars. In due course, it was given to the Newcastle Discovery Museum, where the staff recently discovered that it contained two notes. The first is a brief hand-written obituary of Henry Rolfe, recalling his role at the battles of Vitoria, Toulouse and Waterloo; the second, written by Captain Gordon, records the pocketbook's provenance from Waterloo until it came into his possession in 1895.

Shortly after Corporal Rolfe had taken the Emperor's pocket book, the imperial greatcoat was discovered lying beside *La Dormeuse* by one of Wellington's ADCs, Major the Hon Henry Percy of the 14th Light Dragoons. At Waterloo, Percy was one of only three of Wellington's Staff who was not wounded, although his horse was shot from under him. Wellington therefore selected him to take to London the Waterloo Dispatch (the document announcing the victory) together with the Eagles of the 45th and 105th Infantry Regiments of the Line, and to lay them at the feet of The Prince Regent.

What Percy was careful *not* to lay at The Prince Regent's bulging pumps in

London was Napoléon's greatcoat clasp, which he had cut from the coat that he had found lying on the ground by the abandoned *landau*, where Corporal Rolfe had left it. As with most military greatcoats, the collar of Napoléon's was secured by a snake-link between two bosses, in this case, a pair of gold bees. Like the pocketbook, the gold bee clasp was retained by Henry Percy until his early death in 1825. It can now be seen in the Museum Room at Levens Hall, Cumbria, along with other Waterloo memorabilia that includes an imperial saddle and Wellington's camp bed.

On the day after the battle, while Henry Percy headed for London with the Waterloo Dispatch, the Eagles and the Emperor's bee clasp, Major von Keller was re-united with his spoils of war. Presumably after sorting through the contents of both carriages, he sent Napoléon's hat, sword, and an elaborately embroidered Mameluke burnous to his commander, Marshal Blücher. Found in *La Dormeuse*, and used as a dressing gown by the Emperor, in some accounts this burnous is erroneously referred to as a 'mantle' or a 'mantle of state', which it obviously was not.

Von Keller also sent Blücher the *berline*, in which he had found a large collection of Napoléon's foreign Orders and decorations. To Wellington's considerable irritation, von Keller sent *him* only three minor souvenirs from *La Dormeuse*, including a soiled napkin embroidered with the imperial cypher. This the Iron Duke gave to a Waterloo veteran, for unspecified 'services rendered' in connection with an affair the Duke was pursuing with a certain Mrs Charles Arbuthnot. The grandson of the recipient of this piece of linen later presented it to Madame Tussaud's, along with an account of its acquisition. The napkin was lost in the 1925 fire, but not the correspondence.

While Wellington was grumbling at the slim picking he had been sent by the Prussian Major, Marshal Blücher forwarded Napoléon's hat, sword and decorations to the King Frederick William III of Prussia who, as noted in the introduction, put them on display at the Prussian Hall of Fame in the Zeughaus Museum in Berlin. Blücher then sent the dressing gown to The Prince Regent, and the by-now-empty *berline* to his wife at their house at Kreiblowitz, near Breslau, in what is currently Poland but was then East Prussia. There the *berline* remained until 1973, when Graf (Count) Blücher von Wahlstatt gave it to the Musée National de Malmaison.

In the meantime, von Keller dispatched *La Dormeuse* and the rest of its contents to Düsseldorf where they were put on display from 25th June 1815. The contents in particular attracted a great deal of attention, for they constituted a veritable Aladdin's cave of treasures. Besides an annotated copy of Machiavelli's, *The*

The Mameluke Burnous

Royal Collection Trust © Her Majesty Queen Elizabeth II 2021

[*131*]

Treasures from the *berline* at the Zeughaus Museum, Berlin

Prince, La Dormeuse contained: 'a diamond head dress (tiara), [a] diamond snuff box . . . [and] several boxes of mounted and unmounted diamonds', in addition to the items already described.

After displaying the campaign carriage in Düsseldorf, von Keller took it to London, along with the four remaining horses, Jean Hornn (who had recovered from his wounds), and a second imperial coachman called William Jonsen (who had driven *La Dormeuse* on Elba and during the return to Paris at the start of The Hundred Days, and may have been driving the *berline* at Waterloo).

Once in London, these spoils and the remaining contents of *La Dormeuse*, were 'presented' to The Prince Regent. Accounts differ as to the arrangements of this transfer, variously stating that the campaign carriage was a gift to The Prince Regent from the Prussian government, or was bought from the Prussians by the British government and then given or sold to The Prince Regent. None of these accounts is correct. What actually happened was recorded by William Bullock, in the 1819 sale catalogue of the contents of his museum:

'In consequence of some dispute between the [Prussian] ambassador and the officer [von Keller], who considered the carriage and contents to be his private plunder, The Prince Regent refused to accept them as a present [from the Prussian government] but purchased them of the officer for 3,500 guineas (2020: £378,129) – understanding...

that Mr Bullock had previously offered [von Keller] 2,500 guineas (2020: £245,538), with the intention of exhibiting them to the public. He [The Prince Regent] [then] agreed to part with them [to Mr Bullock] for 3,000 [guineas] (2020: £294,646), one party losing 500 [guineas] (2020: £49,107) and the other advancing 500 [guineas], which offer was accepted by Mr Bullock.'

This rather convoluted transaction between von Keller, The Prince Regent and Bullock, has led to much misunderstanding ever since. Excluded from the deal were the loose diamonds (see below) and the diamond-encrusted snuff box, which Bullock had bought separately from von Keller. This is confirmed by an annotation in the auction catalogue, which states that the snuff box (decorated with one hundred and forty brilliants) was never the property of The Prince Regent. Nonetheless, it was included by Bullock in the 1819 sale when it was bought by a Mr Davies for £166.10.0 (2020: £14,749).

Before any of this happened, and having banked The Prince Regent's cheque, von Keller invested the proceeds in a spa in Breslau and William Bullock collected the carriage and its horses from the Royal Mews, where, since their arrival in London, they had been stabled on the order of Lord Bathurst. This was an arrangement for which Bullock was billed by the Master of the Horse, the Duke of Montrose, 'as His Grace cannot include the [expense] in His Account without an Order from the Treasury' (according to correspondence held in the Letter Books of the Master of the Horse). On payment of the stabling costs incurred at the Royal Mews, Bullock put *La Dormeuse*, the horses, the coachman and the contents on display in his museum on Piccadilly.

It is worth recording here that when von Keller brought the carriage to London but before he sold it to The Prince Regent, he disposed of the loose Napoléonic

Napoléon's Waterloo bicorne hat at the Deutsches Historisches Museum, Berlin

EXHIBITION AT BULLOCKS MUSEUM OF BONEPARTES CARRIAGE TAKEN AT WATERLOO.

La Dormeuse at Bullock's
Museum, 1816

diamonds to a merchant on the Strand named Mawe. Bullock purchased some of these and had one set as a stock pin, which he wore for many years until he sold it, along with a Napoléonic watch, to Madame Tussaud's in 1832 for £50 (2020: £5,724). Von Keller presumably used the proceeds to further defray the cost of his spa.

Once at Bullock's Museum in Piccadilly, the contents of the carriage were arranged in several display cases, and – as in Düsseldorf – the *tout ensemble* created a sensation. Every day, upwards of ten thousand gawpers flocked to see the coach and sit where the Emperor had parked his rump. When the London public had finished admiring *La Dormeuse*, the entire *equipage* went on a tour around the United Kingdom during which more than 800,000 people paid to see it. By the time it returned to London, Mr Bullock had more than offset the purchase price by banking in excess of £33,000 (2020: £2.9 million) from the entry fees, which must have somewhat irked the ever-short-of-cash Prince Regent.

After the UK tour, the four horses were sold at Tattersall's on 1st December

1818, as reported in a clipping from the *Essex County Chronicle* found recently in the Madame Tussaud archives. Sadly, Tattersall's records for the period were destroyed by bombing during the Second World War, so who bought the horses and what was paid for them has been lost. Not so the details of *La Dormeuse* and its contents, which were disposed of at the 1819 auction of Bullock's Museum for a total of £901.6.0 (2021: £79,662), further adding to Mr Bullock's net profit. Mr Bullock's own copy of the sale catalogue still exists and is helpfully annotated by him, in his role as the auctioneer, with the names of the purchasers (Sir Walter Scott and Captain Clark of The Royals, amongst many others) and the prices that they paid. Of particular interest is the following entry, which is repeated elsewhere in the auction catalogue, with the price quoted in guineas:

> 'The two massive Silver Articles of personal convenience, used in the carriage, will be disposed of by Private Contract £31.10.0 (2021: £2,826) [to] The Prince Regent.'

As with the loot taken from Joseph Bonaparte's campaign carriage after Vitoria, these 'articles of personal convenience' were, of course, the aforementioned parcel-gilt silver chamber pots, which were illustrated in two contemporary cartoons. In the one by Rowlandson, one of the potties can clearly be seen being examined by three laughing ladies; in the other cartoon, by Cruickshank, it is in a display case. It is not known what The Prince Regent then did with his newly acquired silver sanitary ware. As the potties do not appear in any current royal inventories, as confirmed by the present Director of the Royal Collection Trust, it is possible that the Prince gave them to his notoriously acquisitive mistress-of-the-moment, Elizabeth, Marchioness Conyngham, or her predecessor, Isabella, Marchioness of Hertford. In any event, after the 1819 auction they disappeared from public view.

Not so *La Dormeuse*, which was bought for £168 (2020: £14,837) at the auction by a Mr Hopkinson, who said he intended to tour it around the USA. The tour never happened and the carriage was sold again to a new owner, who had the same intention. Later, the carriage was seized in lieu of a debt by a carriage maker, Robert Jeffreys of Gray's Inn Road, who in turn sold it in 1842 for £2,500 (2020: £289,100) to Joseph, son of Madame Tussaud. He put it on display at the eponymous waxworks, where it joined Napoléon's Milan Coronation carriage and the coach he had used on St Helena, for which vehicle Madame Tussaud had paid £52 in 1842 (2020: £6,013). There *La Dormeuse* continued to be a significant money-spinner, as part of a special exhibition about Napoléon, advertised as follows in *The Times* in 1843:

above, from top
La Dormeuse at Mme Tussaud's before the fire; the wreckage after the fire; all that remained of *La Dormeuse* – its axle

'Napoléon's celebrated military carriage, taken at Waterloo... his watch, gold snuff box, ring, one of his teeth, the instrument that drew it, tooth-brush, Madras worn in exile, dessert service used by him at St Helens, counterpane stained with his blood... Madame Tussaud & Son's exhibition at the Bazaar, Baker-Street: open from 11 till dusk, and from 7 till 10. Great room, 1s; Napoléon relics and chamber of horrors, 6d.'

The juxtaposition of 'relics' with the 'chamber of horrors' may not be accidental, as Napoléon remained both a revered and a hate figure in British culture for much of the nineteenth century. The 'boneyman' was often substituted for the 'bogeyman' in tales told to frighten children.

In the devastating fire at Madame Tussaud's in 1925, as *The Times* duly reported, the Emperor's campaign carriage was reduced to 'scrap iron', along with the carriage he had used on St Helena, the Milan Coronation coach and the very substantial collection of Napoléonica that the Tussauds had acquired over three generations. So intense was the wax-fuelled fire that the only recognisable remnant of *La Dormeuse* was its main axle, which was displayed once the exhibition was rebuilt and in 1978 lent to Malmaison, where it remains.

Although not directly related to the Emperor's campaign travelling arrangements, this is the appropriate place at which to describe that fire, and list the items from *La Dormeuse*, and other Napoléonica not already mentioned, that were lost in it. As the *Manchester Guardian*'s typically sardonic article recorded:

'Madame Tussaud's, the famous wax-works exhibition in Marylebone Road, London, was badly damaged last night by fire. The fire was discovered shortly after 10.30 [pm]. By 11.30 [pm] the interior of the top storey was a raging furnace. The whole of the roof collapsed with the exception of a dome-like structure at the western end. Scores of fire engines were in attendance, and probably 10,000 people assembled in the neighbourhood. The fire was extinguished by midnight. It was stated that all the Napoléonic relics had been destroyed. The total amount of damage cannot yet be estimated. The whole of the roof and the top floor of the main building was destroyed.

The firemen were greatly handicapped by being unable to get at the hydrants, and there was almost a mile of hose carried in and out of garages and other buildings. The fire brigade was under the command of Mr. A. R. Dyer, who was brought to the scene from a theatre where he had been spending the evening with some friends. Despite the fact that he was in evening dress he took an active part in the operations.

When signs that the outbreak was becoming under control began to be evident the men of the Salvage Corps entered the ground floor and basement of the building. Almost immediately they began to bring out some of the portable property. This at first consisted mainly of pictures of all descriptions. Two of the Salvage Corps men

Fire at Madame Tussaud's, 18th March 1925

below, from top
Napoléon's *necessaire de voyage*
at Madame Tussaud's; Wellington
views Napoléon's death bed
tableau at Mme Tussaud's; The
Elba Flag

were seen struggling along with a huge cage containing a green parrot which after a moment or two hopped on to its perch and began to show signs of a return to perkiness.

The Salvage Corps, after an interval, were able to enter and rescue some of the figures. Members of the crowd inquired after the safety of Charlie Peace, Crippen, and other notorious criminals of the Chamber of Horrors. The sight of the salvage men shouldering the wax models was a strange one.

An eye-witness who lives opposite Madame Tussaud's said in an interview that the fire was a wonderful spectacle. Strong red and golden flames leapt 50 feet from the roof of the building. The wax models could be distinctly heard sizzling.

It is strange to think of the number of eminent, and highly respectable people being burned in effigy in London. Madame Tussaud's famous waxworks spread its net far and wide, and at least forty people of the present Parliament and scores of notabilities outside were represented in wax in these burning galleries. Criminals represented in the Chamber of Horrors, however, will have no feelings in the matter, as they are all dead.'

The Napoléonica destroyed also included relics from HMS *Northumberland*, the ship which conveyed the imperial exile to St Helena; the so-called Elba *drapeau* presented by Napoléon to the Old Guard who had accompanied him in his first exile, which was bought by Madame Tussaud in 1842 for a mere £56 (2020: £6,475); the mattress and pillows from his deathbed, and the bed itself, acquired by Madame Tussaud in the same year but for rather more money: £400 (2020: £46,256), a fact remarked on with surprise in a note in the exhibition's archive; a

right
Bust by Thorwaldsen

roomful of paintings of the Emperor, other members of his family and various Marshals by, amongst others, David and Lefèvre (the fourteen paintings by David – assuming they were genuine – would be worth well in excess of £140 million were they still in existence today, the London art dealer Philip Mould has estimated); a bust of Murat by Rocchi; a bust of Lucien Bonaparte by Trentanove; a plaster bust of Madame Mère; a bust of Napoléon by Bertel Thorvaldsen; the Emperor's gold repeater watch and diamond stock pin, both acquired in 1832 from William Bullock for only £50 (2020: £5,724); a table knife purchased in the Bullock sale, a cameo ring, a pen, a toothbrush, silk stockings and a handkerchief, the tail hair of *Jaffa* (colour not specified, but definitely one of Napoléon's chargers), a clock and a twenty-eight piece china set (from St Helena); locks of Napoléon's and the King of Rome's hair; Napoléon's atlas including several pre-1814 battle plans; a pair of boots, a leather bottle case and several (unspecified) Eagles; his garden chair (again from St Helena); a tooth extracted during the ex-Emperor's final exile; the empty *nécessaire de voyage*, scent bottles and 'other articles' from *La Dormeuse*; a snuff box made from the wood of his original coffin; the sword Napoléon carried in Egypt; and one of his iconic bicorne hats.

Most interesting of all, in the context of this chapter, were the contents of the 'Gillingham Case' in the Napoléon Room at Madame Tussaud's. This housed the items from *La Dormeuse* which Major von Keller had *not* sold to Bullock, but which were acquired by Madame Tussaud from the Major's estate after his death, including:

A rosewood case containing six razors
A silver provisions box (in which von Keller had found the remains of a cold chicken)
A silver goblet, knives and forks all bearing the Imperial arms
A book of post-roads
The Emperor's telescope
Other unspecified silver fittings from the carriage

Given the sums paid for items of Napoléonica at recent auctions, the value today of the lost Tussaud collection is almost incalculable. However, in 1925 Tussaud's insurance claim for the items lost amounted to less than £3,000 (2020: £186,516), which is probably not much more than the cost of any one item in the collection in 2021. Even the Imperial Impresario would be impressed by the net worth of his very own 'bonfire of the vanities'.

below, from top
Napoléon's atlas, telescope
and The Gillingham Case
at Madame Tussaud's

Ein Volk, ein Reich, ein Führer!

MERCHANDISE

'A picture is worth a thousand words'

VEN BEFORE HITLER strutted snarling from the primordial swamp of German nationalism, the creation and distribution of promotional merchandise by an authoritarian regime was not altogether unheard of. Queen Elizabeth I was very adept at projecting her image in paintings that were copied and distributed widely in England. However, Napoléon can rightly claim to be the first to have industrialised the business by deliberate propagation of his image – usually as a soldier or a Roman emperor – in low-cost pictures, engravings, coins, medallions, bronzes, busts and a wide range of ephemera. Even more remarkable than the scale of this Napoléonic enterprise, is the fact that his branded merchandise continued to be manufactured, and added to, after his downfall and death, *and* right up to the present day. What follows is a small but representative selection of just some of it.

Although the First Italian Campaign of 1796–97 and the Egyptian Campaign of 1798–99 generated acres of painted canvas commemorating his victories, both at the time and later, few three-dimensional representations of General Bonaparte were produced. This reflected the fact that, while a hero and emerging as a national figure, nonetheless Napoléon had yet to achieve iconic status. The arrival in Paris of statues and monuments taken during those campaigns, was however reflected in the output of the *bronziers*.

Following the Brumaire coup of 1799, the change from hero to icon began almost overnight as the First Consul's image evolved, changing from the lank-haired revolutionary General to the republican soldier-politician. This portrayal was further enhanced when the First Consul imitated Hannibal by crossing the St Bernard Pass in 1800, albeit on a donkey rather than an elephant. This was an

opposite
Third Reich propaganda poster

Clockwise from top left
General Bonaparte, bronze
statuette*; Bonaparte on a
camel, bronze statuette;
Egyptian obelisk in bronze
on a marble base; Crossing
the St Bernard Pass, bronze
statuette after the painting
by Jacques-Louis David

* The maker and date of manufacture
for all of the items displayed in this
chapter are unknown, unless otherwise
stated in individual captions.

inconvenient fact that, like so many future images, be ruthlessly romanticised with the substitution of a prancing and heroic charger for the humble moke.

The next stage in the development of Napoléon's iconography, as expressed in the mass production of his image, then split onto three parallel tracks. The first, which was the dominant image at the time of the Coronation in 1804, was that of the unmistakeably Roman Emperor. This depiction, based primarily but not exclusively on sculptures by Canova and Chaudet, usually depicted the

Clockwise, from below left
First Consul (late), marble bust;
First Consul (mid-term), gilded bronze silhouette on a marble plaque; First Consul (early), bronze statuette;

Emperor in a deliberately classical manner and often in a classical pose. The inclusion of a laurel wreath crown was frequent, but not invariable, and the mediums of production used in the creation of these souvenirs ranged from gold to abalone, taking in silver, pewter, bronze, wood, copper, ivory, and agate along the way.

Miniatures of the classically-inspired monuments erected on the orders of Napoléon, particularly the Arc de Triomphe de l'Étoile and the Vendôme Column in Paris, were also popular at the time and have been much reproduced since.

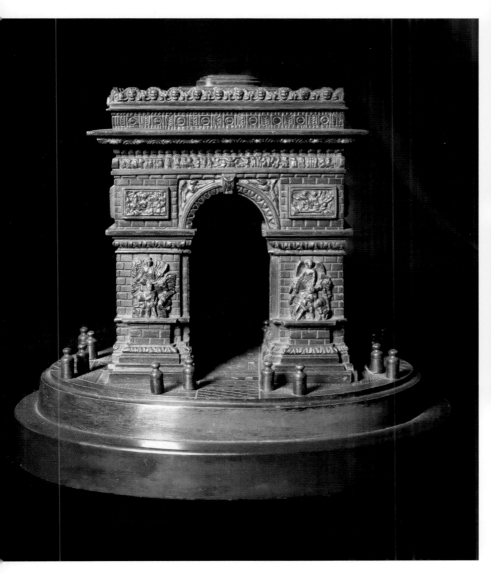

left and above
Arc de Triomphe de l'Étoile, bronze reduction on a marble base; Vendôme Column (1831 version), bronze reduction on a marble base; Vendôme Column, detail showing 1831 statue

clockwise, from below
As the victorious General
(mounted), large bronze model
on Sienna marble base; as the
victorious General (later),
bronze statuette on a marble base;
Napoléon on campaign and in
a contemplative mode, bronze
statuette on a marble base;
as the victorious General (later
mounted) bronze statuette on a
marble base; as the victorious
General, bronze statuette on a
marble base;

The second track, which emerged from the seemingly endless succession of campaigns, was Napoléon as the victorious General, usually depicted in a commanding pose, wearing his iconic hat and greatcoat. The more expensive versions of these models included his horse – and depictions of the Emperor later in his career were not shy of showing his expanding girth or of depicting him in a more contemplative pose.

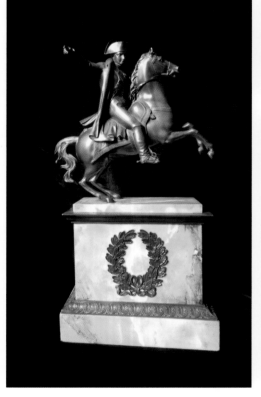

The third track was Napoléon as the soldier-statesman, as opposed to his earlier iconography as a soldier-politician – an important difference. These were less bellicose in their poses, usually hatless and often produced as busts, plaques or as affordable miniature portraits. Equally popular were cheap engravings of the great formal portraits by the Imperial Court painters.

above, from left
As soldier-statesman, oval miniature painting on ivory, unsigned; as soldier-statesman, miniature painting on wood, unsigned; as soldier-statesman, oval miniature painting, unsigned

right
As soldier-statesman, miniature bronze bust; Napoléon in profile, bronze plaque

far right
Napoléon le Grand, contemporary engraving of a painting by Nöel François Bertrand (1784–1852)

The next development in the Napoléonic iconography focussed on promoting the concept of imperial continuity. Although the image of Napoléon's first wife, Joséphine, was depicted in all the usual mediums, both on her own and in profile with her husband, it was the Emperor's second marriage to Marie Louise of Austria, followed by the birth of their son, the King of Rome, which spawned a proliferation of souvenirs designed to show that a new and enduring dynasty had been created.

Napoléon & Marie Louise, pewter medallion by or after Bertrand Andrieu (1761–1822)

The Imperial Family, contemporary hand-coloured engraving on card

LA FAMILLE IMPÉRIALE.

A Paris, chez Osterwald l'ainé, Rue du Pont de Lodi, N° 3.
Déposé à la Direction Générale des Estampes.

With the fall of the First Empire in 1815, the production of merchandise was temporarily halted, but not for long. By the middle of the nineteenth century, the souvenir workshops of Paris and elsewhere were churning out images of the former Emperor not only in his glory, but also in his downfall. The two best known models of this period show the portly and windswept Napoléon gazing out at the South Atlantic, and an ailing, seated man staring defiantly forward, with a map of Europe across his knees. The message of this latter statuette needs no explanation.

below, from left
Napoléon on St Helena, gazing out to sea, bronze statuette on a marble base; *Last Days of Napoléon* by Vincenzo Vela (1820–1891), gilded bronze on a marble base

right
Reduction of monument
in the ambulatory of
Napoleon's tomb in Les
Invalides, gilded and
enamelled bronze on a
marble base

Napoléon's death in 1821, the transfer of his remains from St Helena to Les Invalides in December 1840, and the final entombment of his body in a red quartzite sarcophagus in 1861, all spawned a mass of *in memoriam* imperial memorabilia, often based on the sarcophagus and frequently crafted into a practical product, such as an inkwell.

above, from top
Brass inkwell tomb; Sarcophagus
inkwell, bronze and marble.

The mass manufacture of Napoléonic merchandise in Paris continues unabated, in the form of plastic busts, T-shirts, mugs, postcards and even a watch. While these gewgaws may have little or no investment value, the market in earlier souvenirs continues to boom and provides collectors with real investment growth potential, a fact that would undoubtedly have brought an 'I told you so' smile to Napoléon's (as usually depicted) stern face.

below

Modern souvenir plastic bust;
modern souvenir T-shirt;
Napoléonic watch *c.* 2021

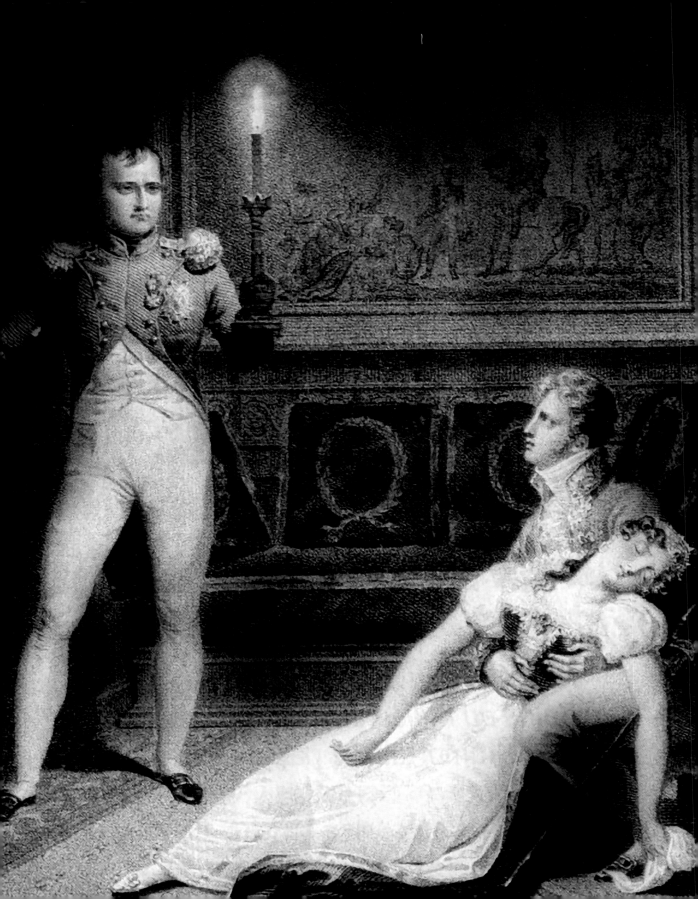

COLLECTABLES

'Not tonight, Joséphine'

NLIKE THE OTHER Napoléonic quotes in this book, the words that sub-title this chapter's heading were never actually spoken by, or directly attributed to, the Emperor. In fact, they were first spoken in *The Royal Divorce*, a play by the Irish dramatist, novelist and painter, W G Wills, and G G Collingham, the pseudonym of the London playwright, Mary Helen White. The curtain on this melodrama rose on 1st May 1891, but not many times thereafter. The words were used again as part of the title of George Mahood's travelogue, *Not Tonight, Joséphine: A Road Trip Through Small-Town America*, first published in 2016. These literary and musical creations make a point. Many decades after his fall from power, not only do Napoléon's relics continue to fascinate, but so too does his love life.

In this he is not alone, for he shares with past and present stars of stage and screen a rampant public curiosity, not only about his sex life, but also about his sexuality and his physical manhood. As evidence of this prurient interest in celebrities, debate still continues on the actual sexuality of Vaslav Nijinsky, Rudolph Valentino, and Cary Grant, to name but a few; although not about Valentino's manhood which, like those of Charlie Chaplin and Roscoe 'Fatty' Arbuckle, was said to be on an imperial scale. By contrast, no such doubt – but plenty of curiosity – still exists about the gay sex life of Sergei Diaghilev, Freddie Mercury and Rock Hudson, and the extent of the sapphic encounters of Greta Garbo, Judy Garland and Marlene Dietrich. These examples are but the tip of a resolutely tumescent fascination with what goes on behind the bedroom doors of the stars.

Where Napoléon is concerned, and as with some of the Hollywood greats, it does not seem to matter that plenty of factual evidence exists to show that he

Rudolph Valentino as *The Sheikh*

opposite
'Not tonight, Joséphine'

[*153*]

was no monk. As Andrew Roberts confirms in his book, *Napoléon the Great*, the First Consul's highly sexualised letters to Joséphine from the Italian Campaign, in one of which he urges her not to wash ahead of his return to the marital bed, demonstrate that there was no lack of libido in his first marriage. The birth of his son, the King of Rome, confirms that the Emperor's second marriage was not chaste either. Nor was his extra-marital sex life, before and after his second marriage. The existence of several mistresses, of whom the best known are Comtesse Marie Walewska and Eléonore Denuelle de la Plaigne, further affirms this assumption, as does their imperially acknowledged offspring: Comte Alexandre Colonna-Walewski and Comte Charles Léon, both of whom bore a strong resemblance to the Emperor. As additional evidence of his paternity, a recent DNA test of a lineal descendant of Alexandre, when compared to that of a descendant of Jérôme Bonaparte, has confirmed it.

above, from left
Comtesse Marie Walewska (1786–1817); Comte Alexander Colonna-Walewski (1810–1868); Raza Roustam (1783–1845); General Duroc (1772–1813)]

However, in his 1981 book, *Mars Without Venus*, Major General Frank Richardson DSO OBE MD posits the self-contradictory theory that Napoléon was both impotent and bisexual. To prove the latter, he cites the close relationship between Napoléon and one of his Mameluke bodyguards, Raza Roustam, stating that it was more than one of master and servant. It is certainly true that Napoléon 'acquired' the nineteen-year-old Georgian slave during the Egyptian Campaign when he was given the handsome youth by Sheikh Khalil el Bakri in 1799. It is also true that the Mamelukes were initially an unmarried warrior caste, perpetuated through the purchase of slave boys seized from Georgia by Arab slavers. However, by Napoléon's time most Mamelukes were married, their power was dynastic and Raza Roustam married Alexandrine Doudeauville, daughter of Empress Joséphine's *valet de chambre*, in 1806.

This allegation, and similar assertions about the Emperor's relationship with his tousle-haired ADC, General Géraud Duroc, and with Emperor Alexander I of Russia, are based on speculation, Bourbon *émigrés*' malicious gossip, and a misunderstanding of nineteenth-century expressions of emotion. An uninformed reading of the letters between King Ludwig II of Bavaria and Richard Wagner would lead to the conclusion that the two enjoyed a passionate, physical relationship, which they did not.

Whether or not Napoléon was bisexual – and the dubious evidence for the theory advanced by Richardson is not even circumstantial – history continues to assume that he was not much of a lover. This belief is under-pinned by another of his mistresses, the actress Marguerite Georges, who shared with the opera diva, Giuseppina Grassini, the distinction of having had sex with both Napoléon and Wellington. Grassini never spoke of the affairs, but Georges was less discreet. When asked who was better between the sheets, the actress replied: '*Monsieur le Duc, il était de beaucoup le plus fort.*' It is worth noting that the word '*fort*' has a number of meanings depending on the context including 'strong', 'stiff', 'fierce' and 'large', so it may refer to the size of the two military commanders' *bijoux de famille*. Whether Madame Georges was referring to technique or size is now anyone's guess. Or is it, at least as regards the ducal and imperial *membrum virile*?

Marguerite Georges
(787–1867)

In the case of Wellington, who was a notorious philanderer, there is some evidence that his bedroom equipment was more than adequate, as shown at the unveiling of the Wellington Monument at Hyde Park Corner in 1822. Sculpted by Richard Westmacott (from 1837 Sir Richard), and based on one of the figures of the Horse Tamers on the Quirinal Hill in Rome, the statue has a facial profile modelled on that of the Duke himself. It was the first male nude to be put on public display in London since Roman times. Despite the fact that the statue had been funded to the sum of £10,000 (2020: £1,300,000) by a prim group of upper-class women known as the Ladies of England, the proportionally modelled flaccid phallus and ample scrotum caused such moral outrage that a sizeable fig leaf had to be bolted into place soon after the Union flag had been tugged away to reveal the statue in all its glory.

Giuseppina Grassini
(1773–1850)

Despite this prudery, much controversy still resulted and a cartoon of the statue by George Cruickshank, entitled *Backside and Front View of the Ladies Fancy Man, Paddy Carey*, was published in July 1822. In it, a crowd of spectators are admiring the statue of 'O'Killus Esq – Erected in Hide [*sic*] Park, in Honor [*sic*] of the Waterloo Man & his Soger Men'. Speech bubbles above the crowd include comments such as:

Cruickshank's cartoon of the Wellington Monument

'Do you think it will stand the weather?'

'Bless you, it will stand anything; My eyes, what a size!'

'La! They must be a brazen set of jades to stick up such a thing [slang for penis] in public – what is it meant for?'

'I understand it is intended to represent His Grace after bathing in the Serpentine and defending himself from an attack of Constables'.

Only one wholly nude, full-length representation of Napoléon exists (the rest all have integrated fig leaves), and it is in the Bernard Ledoux Collection. A bronze reduction of a marble statue by Antonio Canova, now in the Duke of Wellington's London home, Apsley House, it depicts Napoléon as *Mars the Peacemaker*. Napoléon sat in Paris for a portrait bust by Canova in 1802, but the *Mars* was sculpted in Rome between 1803 and 1806, so not from life.

That Canova's representation of the size of the imperial wedding tackle may be unintentionally accurate is confirmed by the account of the *post mortem* made on the exile's body by Dr Walter Henry, an English medic who took notes at Napoléon's autopsy. The procedure, which was performed at the late Emperor's request as he feared that his cause of death was hereditary, was presided over by Dr Francis Burton, the Regimental Surgeon of the 66th Regiment of Foot (the

 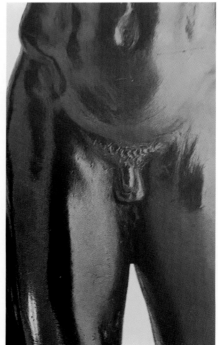

right and detail
Canova's *Mars the Peacemaker*

unit tasked with guarding Napoléon on St Helena), and five other British doctors including Dr Henry. It was, however, actually performed by Napoleon's personal physician, Dr François Carlo Antommarchi. Dr Henry wrote in cod-Latin (here translated) of the 'remarkably small male parts, like those of a boy' and then later, more anatomically and in English, 'the penis and testicles were very small'. Further evidence as to the size of the imperial equipment is provided by a grisly, shrivelled relic which has been in the private collection of the late American urologist, Dr John K Lattimer, since 1977. He added it to Hermann Goering's last-worn under-wear and one of his two cyanide capsules, President Lincoln's blood-stained collar worn on the night of his assassination, and bloody upholstery from the car in which President Kennedy was shot. According to the notorious Holly-wood private investigator, Fred Otash, JFK shared at least one characteristic with the Imperial Impresario: he was, apparently, 'hung like a cashew'.

How Napoléon's principal asset joined this cabinet of creepy curiosities is described by General Richardson. According to his research, it was Dr Antom-marchi who removed Napoléon's penis during the autopsy on the billiard table at Longwood. Precisely what happened to it next is unclear to Richardson, who nevertheless asserts that at some point it was disposed of in two pieces, with the foreskin ending up in the Casa Museo Mario Pratz at 1 via Zanardelli, in Rome; how it got there is not explained. Meanwhile, so Richardson states, the circum-cised *membrum* was offered for sale, as part of the Vignali Collection, by Sotheby's (actually it was sold at Christie's) on 29th October 1969 at which time it was bought by Dr Lattimer. For the most part, this account is fanciful and Richardson's reliance on hearsay rather than fact undermines further his theory as to the Emperor's sexuality.

The truth is that, during the *post mortem*, Dr Antommarchi was authorised by Dr Burton to remove some intestinal tissue and the late exile's heart and stomach. The former ended up in the Hunterian Museum in London, and was destroyed by bombing in the Second World War, and the organs were sealed in jars that were placed inside the coffin. Dr Antommarchi, however, did *not* remove his penis – that was done by Napoléon's personal chaplain, the Abbé Ange Paul Vignali.

As well as being a priest, who was later murdered in a vendetta, Vignali had medical training and, with the assistance of Napoléon's Mameluke valet, Ali (Louis-Étienne) Saint Denis, who recorded the event in his memoirs, published in 1826, it was Vignali who severed the organ while the corpse was being dressed and before it was encased in a series of caskets. The relic remained in the Vignali family's collection of Napoléonica until it was sold by the priest's nephew to the London bookdealer, Maggs Bros, in 1916. There it was held until 1924, when Maggs sold the entire Vignali Collection to an American antiquarian bookseller,

Dr Antommarchi (1780–1838)

above, from left
Uriah Maggs (1828– 1913);
The case containing Napoléon's
petite baguette

Dr Abraham Rosenbach of Philadelphia, for £400 (2020: £24,868). The American had the 'mummified tendon', as it was described in his New York exhibition catalogue of 1924, mounted in a gold-tooled morocco leather case. A journalist who attended the exhibition wrote of seeing two women giggling, as they viewed 'something that looked like a maltreated strip of buckskin or shrivelled eel'.

In 1947, the Vignali Collection was acquired in its entirety from Rosenbach by the American collector, Donald Hyde, and then sold after his death in 1966 to another American dealer called Bruce Gimelson, who paid US$35,000 (2020: £438,000) for it. In 1972, Gimelson offered the collection, at cost, as a single lot at Christie's in London, but failed to find a buyer. Five years later the collection was dispersed at an auction at Druot in Paris, at which Dr John Lattimer paid today's equivalent of £56,000 just for the penile relic.

The Emperor's penis was later reported on in 2008 by Tony Perrottet, who describes it in his book, *Napoléon's Privates*, as 'like a piece of beef jerky … very small, very shrivelled, about an inch-a-half long'. This is hardly surprising, and not exactly conclusive as to the scale of the Emperor's deflated impregnator during his lifetime. Anyone who has either viewed a desiccated corpse, or observed the often-remarkable difference in size between an erect and a flaccid *petite baguette*, will understand this point. Nonetheless, whatever its original dimension, were it ever to be offered on the open market by the present owner, the late Dr Lattimer's daughter who keeps it in a suitcase away from public view, the air-dried appendage would – assuming it could be verified as being what it purports to be – command a price well in excess of the £1,500,000 paid in 2014 for one of Napoléon's bicorne hats, thereby proving that size does not always matter.

As for the undergarment which housed the imperial appendage, despite the huge quantities of linen owned by Napoléon, examples of his undershorts are in short supply. One pair of 'Cashimeer [*sic*] small-clothes' (i.e., underpants) were among the items of clothing in *La Dormeuse* that were offered for sale in the Bullock auction (Lot 99) on Friday 11th June 1819; they sold to a Mr Shipley for £1.18.0 (2020: £169). Even at today's values, this is considerably less than a pair of Napoléon's silk drawers worn on St Helena, which were auctioned by Osenat in 2014 with a pre-sale estimate of €15,000-20,000. Most of this imperial linen was made by Mademoiselles L'Olive and de Beuvry, who in their memoirs recorded that they delivered two hundred and forty muslin shirts to the Imperial wardrobe between January and April 1813 alone.

One of Napoléon's shirts

In the inventory taken after Napoléon's death, a mere forty-seven shirts were recorded, most of which he had bequeathed to his family and staff. Some of these shirts, along with other monogrammed and coroneted hosiery, underwear, nightwear and linen, are held in public and private collections, and occasionally come up for sale. Given the vast quantity of imperial linen extant in 1815, it is worth noting that the Bullock auction in 1819 included only two pairs of imperial white silk stockings, three cambric shirts, a black stock, one muslin and four cambric handkerchiefs, and a pair of braces, all of which were found in *La Dormeuse*. They sold to individual curio seekers for a combined value of £22 (2020: £1,972).

Just under two hundred years later, in 2014, a sweat-stained cotton nightshirt, worn by Napoléon as he lay dying, and two sleeves from the nightshirt that the imperial exile was wearing when he actually died on 5th May 1821, were estimated to sell respectively for €40,000 (£34,188) and €18,000 (£15,384). These items came from the collection of Achille Archambault, one of Napoléon's former coachmen, who accompanied him to St Helena as head groom, and who later labelled them:

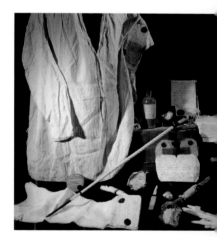

The Archambault collection

> 'This shirt was removed from the Emperor Napoléon the 4 May 1821. As the Emperor's linen was bleached at my home, I gave the order to the staff responsible for this to give it to me and only me, the last items taken from His Majesty.'

Archambault was one of those who assisted with the *post mortem* arrangements. When the ex-Emperor's remains were returned to France in 1840, it was Archambault who led Napoléon's dapple-grey charger, *Sheikh*, behind the funeral car. In the meantime, he was offered F100,000 (2020: £277,000) for his collection, but turned it down, and kept the items as heirlooms for his family. They were only rediscovered in 2014, lying in a dusty box in Corsica. However, when the collection was offered for sale by Osenat, a descendant of Archambault objected on the grounds that the items were of such historical importance that any risk they might leave France had to be blocked. The auction house concurred, and the entire Archambault collection was withdrawn, although a pair of Napoléon's white silk stockings, with an Archambault provenance, sold at Osenat's Bicentennial sale in April 2021 (Lot 203) for €9,200 (£7,820).

Still on the theme of the ex-Emperor's linen, three single coloured and a pair of white silk stockings, a cotton *chausette*, a cotton batiste shirt (worn on St Helena and bequeathed to General Bertrand), and a printed cotton neck scarf, were sold in the Monaco Collection auction in 2014 for €146,000 in total (£124,786). The shirt alone sold for £59,829, with the coloured stockings reappearing on the market for a second time as Lot 200 at the Osenat Bicentennial sale with a pre-sale estimate of €12,000 (£10,256). They sold on this occasion for €21,500 (£18,275), while at the same auction Lot 182, a single, embroidered handkerchief of Napoléon's, sold for an impressive €15,000 (£12,750); a bloodstained bandage used at his *post mortem* sold for €27,000 (£22,950); and – most eye-watering of all – a shirt worn by him 'after Waterloo' (Lot 199) sold for €80,000 (£68,000).

It is interesting to speculate the prices that might have been achieved at this auction for the Napoléon's stock worn at Waterloo, and a collection of his underwear and a cotton scarf worn by him on St Helena, all of which he bequeathed to Lucien Bonaparte and were later acquired by Madame Tussaud at the auction of Lucien's estate – only to be burnt to a cinder in 1925.

*   *   *

Napoléon's desiccated penis and his assorted linen are by no means the only pieces of ephemera of no intrinsic value associated with the Emperor that remain desirable and which command high prices. Another example of Napoléonic collectables are his teeth. Like all modern celebrities, but without the aid of sophisticated orthodontistry, he took great care of his teeth (as well as the rest of his body). This was unlike King Ludwig II of Bavaria, who lost all his front teeth at an early age from eating too many sweets, or Ludwig's cousin, the Empress Elizabeth ('Sisi') of Austria, whose teeth were stained black by the mercury she took to combat the syphilis with which she had been infected by her husband, Emperor Franz Josef I. The reports of Sisi holding a fan in front of her face when she spoke was not because of an innate shyness, as is widely believed, but from vanity. Sisi's daily grooming routine took all morning, including three hours dedicated to combing and braiding her hair, and the three-weekly washing with raw egg and brandy which took all day.

Napoléon was an habitually early riser (usually at 2 am). He spent the early hours working with his personal staff, before taking a hot bath in which he would lie for up to two hours, while dictating orders and instructions. This was followed by a cup of tea and his *toilette*, which included scraping his tongue, brushing his teeth, and shaving himself. Then, after a second bath, he liberally doused his body with Eau de Cologne, up to sixty bottles of which he used every month. According to research recently published by Professor Parvez Haris of De Montfort University, this excessive use could have caused the gastric cancer from which the Emperor eventually died.

Napoléon's ablutions were assisted by his Mameluke servants and his valet-in-waiting, and facilitated with beautifully crafted accessories. By 1815, there existed at least five large and ten small *nécessaires de voyage* containing his *toilette* equipment, and two containing dental instruments, made by French goldsmith Martin-Guillame Biennais. This accounts for the relatively large number of Napoléonic razors, shaving soap boxes and brushes, tongue scrapers, scent bottles, and tooth brushes that are in public and private collections. Three silver-handled tooth brushes, and a silver box containing tooth-cleaning powder, were

One of Napoléon's five large *nécessaires de voyage*

Dr Barry O'Meara (1786–1836)

An imperial toothbrush

found by Major von Keller in *La Dormeuse* after Waterloo, and were sold in four separate lots at Bullock's auction in 1819 for a total of £9.18.11 (2020: £890). One of the dental-care kits by Biennais, thought also to have been acquired by von Keller with *La Dormeuse* but not sold to The Prince Regent, is now in the Fondation Napoléon Collection, having in the meantime been held by the Rothschild family. A small Biennais *necessaire*, including yet another silver-handled toothbrush, is in the same collection. It was not taken at Waterloo, but was given to Napoléon's secretary, Comte Emmanuel de Las Cases, on St Helena, with the words that it had been used by the donor on the morning of the Battle of Austerlitz.

Napoléon's obsessive attention to his oral and bodily cleanliness did not prevent him from getting severe toothache during his second exile, which resulted in three of his wisdom teeth being extracted by Dr Barry O'Meara. He was the exile's British-appointed Irish physician, who later criticised his patient's treatment on St Helena, both in letters to the Admiralty and in his book, *Napoléon in Exile, or A Voice from St Helena*, published in 1822. This criticism resulted in his removal from the island in 1818 and the arrival of Dr Antommarchi. According to Madame Tussaud's 1901 catalogue:

'On visiting Italy [after Napoléon's death] the doctor [O'Meara] gave one of these relics [the teeth] to Madame Mère, another to the ex-King of Spain, Joseph Bonaparte, and the last he kept for himself. This, together with the instrument with which the teeth were extracted, was sold at the sale of Prince Lucien Bonaparte's effects by Mr Robins, the famous auctioneer, and was purchased by Madame Tussaud and Sons'.

Lucien Bonaparte, a younger brother of Napoléon and Joseph, died in 1840. At the time, George Henry Robins was in business in Covent Garden as an auctioneer. The auction house originally belonged to his father, Henry, but George Robins ran it from 1798 and was active in the business until his demise in 1847. Presumably, the Bonaparte sale took place at some point between 1840 and 1847. During this same period Robins, whose estate was valued on his death at £154,000 (2020: £16,338,128), was also the auctioneer who sold the famous Horace Walpole Collection at Strawberry Hill House in a twenty-four-day sale that raised £29,615 (2020: £3,424,700). The Strawberry Hill auction catalogue survives in the Paul Mellon Centre for Studies in British Art, but not that of the Bonaparte auction, which is a pity as it would have been interesting to know the price that Tussaud's paid for the imperial molar.

* * *

Although not exactly a body part, locks of Napoléon's hair are equally desirable and more readily available than imperial teeth for collectors. This is partly because he freely gave away his hair as gifts. He also instructed his valet, Marchand, not only to send the lock of hair belonging to his son, the King of Rome, to his family, but also to distribute, *post mortem*, clumps of his own hair to his mother and siblings, and to his suite-in-waiting on St Helena. This instruction was carried out, and a lock of his master's hair retained by Marchand was later given by him to a friend, who in turn sold it to Madame Tussaud's; it, too, went up in smoke in 1925.

Fortunately, many other imperial follicles survive, including a plait of hair contained in a cameo locket, which is in the Royal Collection Trust (RCIN: 71216), and two locks of the Emperor's hair in the National Army Museum's collection. One of these (a *post mortem* lock) was given by Marchand to Major (later Major General) Anthony Emmett, who commanded the Royal Engineers detachment on St Helena. Emmett's grandson gave it to the Royal United Services Museum, whose collection was transferred to the National Army Museum in London, when it opened in 1971. The other lock, possibly preserved by the valet after giving his imperial master a haircut, was given by Marchand to Captain T W Poppleton RN, during the naval officer's visit to St Helena in 1817.

Lock of Napoléon's hair

Royal Collection Trust © Her Majesty
Queen Elizabeth II 2021

Betsy Balcombe (1802–1871)
with Napoléon

Sir John Soane's Museum ring
with Napoléon's hair

Napoléon also gave a small bunch of hair to the young Elizabeth 'Betsy' Balcombe some time before his death. Betsy was the daughter of William Balcombe, an East India Company official and one of the civil administrators on St Helena. She gave the hair to the architect, Sir John Soane, who had it encased in a mourning ring. After Sir John's death in 1837 the ring disappeared, only to resurface in 2009 when it was bought back by his museum for £41,000. That was rather more than the £8,600 paid at a New Zealand auction in the same year for a small tuft of Napoléon's hair, cut from his head after his death. It was sold by the descendants of Denzil Ibbetson, a civil engineer on the British staff in St Helena.

If the price paid by the Soane Museum sounds high, then it is worth noting that a *single* strand of Napoléon's hair, attached by sealing wax to a piece of paper on which was written 'A Single Hair of Napoléon Bonaparte's head 29th Augt 1816', sold at auction in 2015 for £130. The Emperor's former aide, the Comte de Flahaut, once famously remarked that he had 'seen enough hair since Napoléon's death to carpet the floor of Versailles'. Nevertheless, further evidence of the value of the Imperial Impresario's 'barnet' is provided by the prices paid for Lots 87 and 176 at the sale of the Monaco Collection on Sunday 16th November 2014.

General Bertrand

The first lot, with a pre-sale estimate of €1,500-2,000, consisted of a glazed reliquary frame containing two locks of hair, one belonging to the First Consul and the other to Joséphine. Napoléon had given this to General Bertrand in early-1804, along with a piece of fabric assumed to be stained with the consular blood, although how and why was not explained in the catalogue entry. It sold for €10,500 (£12,285). The second lot included two whisps of hair belonging to the Emperor and his second Empress (so, post-1804), with their authenticity affirmed by Bertrand's grandson, Henri. The pre-sale estimate for this lot was €2–3,000 and the hammer price was €8,500 (£9,945). A similar price was also paid in 2015 for a substantial lock of imperial hair, given to Admiral George Brine RN at St Helena in 1816, which was offered at auction for £800-1,200 and sold for £7,500. This price was exceeded in 2020 by yet another lock of *post mortem* Napoléonic hair, which sold at auction in New Zealand for £12,500. It was accompanied by a handwritten note stating that it had come from Jean Abram Navarre, a Swiss-born servant of Napoléon.

* * *

The public's fascination with the sexual proclivities, body parts (intimate and otherwise), and the underwear of the great and the good is only matched by their morbid interest in death, and their willingness to pay considerable sums for collectables associated with celebrity demises, funerals and interments.

Although there is no hard evidence for the legend that the sailors on HMS *Victory* drank the brandy in which Nelson's body had been preserved on the journey from Trafalgar to Gibraltar, the story persists. It is true, however, that the two Union flags and the White Ensign from his flagship, flown on the stern of his nautically-themed funeral car, were shredded and distributed by the naval bearer party before they could be consigned to the Admiral's final place of rest, in a sarcophagus under the dome in St Paul's Cathedral. When, as occasionally happens, these bits of flag come on the market they are bid for hotly. In 2016 a tiny piece sold for £8,125, while a much larger fragment sold in 2018 for £300,000. The value of the bullet that killed Nelson at Trafalgar, and his bloodstained uniform coat, will never be known as they are held in the Royal Collection and the National Maritime Museum at Greenwich respectively. The latter also has a fragment of the black velvet and the ship's figurehead used on his funeral car, which is all that remain of the vehicle.

Nelson's funeral car

The death of Napoléon, 5th May 1821

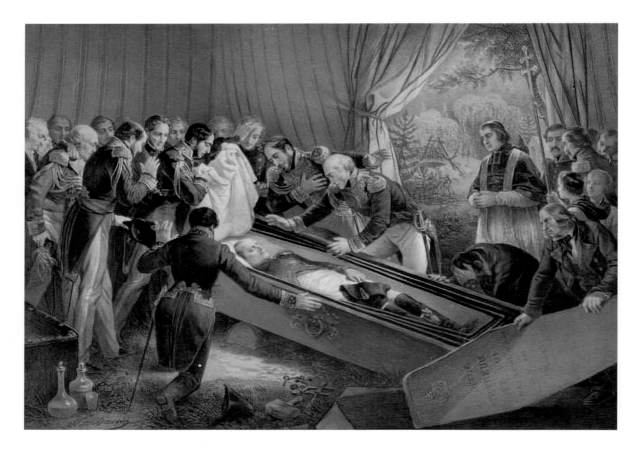

Napoléon exhumed, showing the
outer casket, 14th October 1840

However, the actual coffins in which the famous dead are consigned to the
earth, or to a marble sarcophagus, are generally beyond the reach of collectors.
Not so the black silk lining of Napoléon's grave, and his original outer coffin.
These became available when the ex-Emperor's body was exhumed on St
Helena on 14th October 1840, prior to the return of his remains to France and a
State Funeral in Paris in December of that year. Although the wood of the outer
mahogany casket was in good condition, it had to be cut away to allow full
access to the lead, wood and tin coffins within, and from it was made, *inter alia*,
a snuff box. Meanwhile, when the inner coffin was finally opened, Napoléon's
body was reported by the Abbé Félix Cocquereau to be 'covered in a light foam'
due to putrefaction, but was otherwise remarkably well preserved: it was
exposed for only a few minutes and not examined. Unfortunately, like Napoléon's tooth, his hair and much else besides, the snuff box and the grave lining
were destroyed in the fire at Madame Tussaud's in 1925, and neither a description
nor a photograph survives.

The second known piece of the mahogany outer coffin, which may have been acquired by the Royal United Services Museum at the sale of John Davis Sainsbury's Napoléonica collection in 1845 (to be considered later in this chapter), is described in the RUSI catalogue of 1920 simply as a 'fragment of the Coffin of Napoléon I'. For some reason, it does not currently feature in the National Army Museum's online inventory. Charlotte Brontë is recorded as receiving a piece from her tutor, Monsieur Heger, and there is one further piece of the coffin in Sens, France. It was given to the town by Napoléon's Mameluke servant, Ali Saint Denis, who was present at the exhumation in October 1840. He also bequeathed to the town, where he lived from 1827 until his death in 1856, some books annotated by Napoléon and a cockade from one of his bicorne hats.

By comparison with the paucity of fragments still in existence of Napoléon's original outer coffin, there are many extant examples of his death mask, although there is considerable debate and dispute about the facts relating to where and when they were cast. The problems arise from the event at which the original mould was created. The day after Napoléon died, the aforementioned *post mortem* was conducted. What happened next was recorded by Dr Antommarchi:

'After I had finished the autopsy, I made room for the *valet de chambre*, who dressed the body as the Emperor was usually dressed [in the uniform of a Colonel of the Chasseurs à Cheval of the Imperial Guard] during his life... Thus dressed, Napoléon was, at a quarter past six, removed from the drawing room [other accounts state that the *post mortem* was carried out in the billiard room, which was next door and the more likely venue given the convenient height of the billiard table], into which the crowd immediately entered. The sheet and linen that had been used in the dissection of the body were carried away, torn in pieces and distributed; they were stained with blood, and everyone, therefore, wished to have a fragment of them.'

Some of these gruesome relics ended up in the Ledoux Collection and the (now lost) collection at Madame Tussaud's. However, unlike Nelson's flags, these souvenirs of Napoléon's death do not currently command huge prices; the last piece of the sheet to have been sold (in 2018) achieved only £180, despite its authenticated provenance.

At some point during the *post mortem* – probably once the examination had been completed, but before the body was handed over to be dressed by Ali Saint Denis and vandalised by the Abbé Vignali – a death mask mould or matrix was made by Dr Burton. Some accounts allege that the mask was made the following day and that the face had started to decompose, but this seems unlikely given the Abbé Cocquereau's 1840 report that the body, which had not been embalmed,

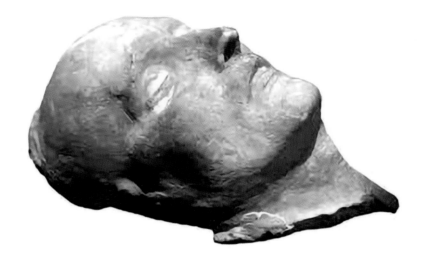

Napoléon's death mask (face only), Antommarchi model, now in the Musée de l'Armée in Paris

showed almost no signs of decomposition when exhumed. In any event, as (according to data on the *Napoléon.org* website) there was no Plaster of Paris on the island, Dr Burton had to make-do with gypsum from a deposit in the south of St Helena. The key difference between the materials is that while both have similar moulding properties, they have different chemical compositions. Using the gypsum, and in order to create as full a record as possible of the imperial features, Dr Burton made several moulds from different parts of the late Emperor's head, including a single mould of the face. All of these he left to dry on a marble mantlepiece, although whether in the billiard room or the drawing room is uncertain as both had large fireplaces. What happened next remains in dispute amongst historians and antiquarians, and will probably never be resolved.

According to Dr Burton, Fanny Bertrand, the wife of the General Henri Bertrand, stole the facial imprint, leaving behind the moulds for the neck, chin, ears and back of the head, and then gave the vital component to Dr Antommarchi. This she denied, and Dr Burton failed in a later court case to recover it. At the same time, Antommarchi contended that Dr Burton had made a copy of the original facial cast and had given it to him. If Dr Burton was right then, in the immortal words of Mandy Rice-Davis, '[Antommarchi] would have said that, wouldn't he?'. Given that no Burton-created casts apparently exist, the weight of evidence would seem to favour his contention that the original mould was indeed stolen from the fireplace, either by Madame Bertrand and/or by Antommarchi.

Whatever the truth of the matter, it appears that Antommarchi started making copies of the ear-less, face-only death mask both in plaster and in bronze from a date after 1828. These, in turn, were used as models from which additional masks were manufactured by other and later hands, including an 1833 subscription series, signed by Antommarchi and cast by L. Richard et E. Quesnel of Paris. Clearly, those made from the original mould are both the most collectable and the most valuable, provenance being everything when it comes to value.

In the case of Napoléon's death mask, establishing provenance has created many problems, although the so-called Bertrand Mask, now at the Château de Malmaison, is thought to have been made for Madame Bertrand in London in 1821 from the original impression. The Antommarchi-Azhemar Mask, also now at Malmaison, and the example in the Ledoux Collection which uniquely has a gilt bronze wreath and is numbered '2', are almost certainly Antommarchi originals. Additional contenders for this accolade include those in the collections of the Auckland Art Gallery, a plaster example in the Library of North Carolina, and the bronze version in the Louisiana State Museum. Other examples, including those in the National Museums Liverpool, the Napoléon Museum in Cuba, and the Musée de l'Armée in Paris, are probably later castings, possibly made from copies of the original mould.

The last plaster death mask with an early casting date to have been sold on the open market, known as the 'Boys Cast', was bought at Bonhams in 2013 for £170,000, while a bronze version dated 1833 (from the Quesnel foundry) was sold in the 2014 Monaco Collection auction for only €5,000 (2020: £4,270). This difference in values underlines the importance of provenance and date to the value. Given the controversy over the original mould or matrix, it is worth recording in full the entry for the Boys Cast in the Bonhams' catalogue:

Death mask of Napoléon, taken on the Island of St Helena on 7 May 1821, two days after his death, cast in plaster [*sic*] and presented to the Rev Richard Boys, Senior Chaplain of St Helena, with an autograph note of authentication by him, written prior to his departure from the island in 1829: 'This Cast was taken from the Face of Napoléon Buonaparte as he lay dead at Longwood St. Helena 7th May 1821 which I do hereby certify/ R. Boys M.A. Sen.r Chaplain/ By Rubidge'; the inside of the cast inscribed in pencil 'Rev Mr Boys'; on a mahogany stand of *c.* 1830, to which the note is affixed, in white plaster of Paris, incorporating an internal plaited rope for suspension, exterior with a fine and varied aged patina, including normal minor wear, glass dome and one foot of the stand lacking, 317 × 155 mm, [cast for the Rev Richard Boys by Joseph William Rubidge on St Helena in May or June 1821]

Footnotes

NAPOLÉON'S DEATH MASK, CAST FOR THE REV RICHARD BOYS, WITH A NOTE OF AUTHENTICATION WRITTEN BY HIM IN HIS CAPACITY AS SENIOR CHAPLAIN ON ST HELENA. The mask was made by, or was the gift of, the portrait-painter Joseph William Rubidge, and therefore must have come into Boys's possession prior to Rubidge's departure from St Helena in June 1821, and very probably before 27 May when his colleague Dr Francesco Antommarchi left the island, taking the moulds of the mask with him.

IT IS, WE BELIEVE, THE MOST SIGNIFICANT EXAMPLE OF NAPOLÉON'S DEATH MASK REMAINING IN PRIVATE HANDS, AND INDUBITABLY ONE OF ONLY A TINY HANDFUL WITH A PROVENANCE LINKING IT DIRECTLY TO ST HELENA.

This catalogue entry is important for a number of reasons. First, it is unclear as to the precise material of the Boys Mask: the word 'plaster' could apply to either gypsum or Plaster of Paris (if it is made of the latter, then it seems unlikely but not impossible that it was cast on St Helena). Second, the catalogue appears to be at odds with the facts asserted in the court case between Burton and Madame Bertrand as to what happened to the original mould. Finally, it may be inconsistent with the following entry in the Christie's 1969 sale catalogue of the Vignali Collection, which is itself at varying degrees of variance with other accounts, particularly as it states that the mould was made by Antommarchi rather than by Dr Burton:

A DEATH MASK OF NAPOLÉON FROM THE MATRIX MOULDED AT ST HELENA BY NAPOLÉON'S DOCTOR, ANTOMMARCHI.

This matrix Antommarchi retained till 1833 [*sic*], when he made and issued a few masks made from it each bearing his stamp at the base (the matrix was then handed to the French Government and is now in the Hôtel des Invalides, Paris). THIS MASK IS OF EXCEPTIONAL INTEREST, BEING THE ONE OWNED [*sic*] BY NAPOLÉON'S CHAPLAIN, WHO ADMINISTERED THE LAST SACRAMENT TO NAPOLÉON AT ST HELENA.

In any event, after the sale at Bonhams in 2013 the export of the Boys Mask was blocked by the UK's Department of Culture, Media and Sport, but was lifted in March 2014 when doubt was cast on the mask's authenticity. In this whole saga, the only undisputed fact would appear to be that the truth will never be known. For those interested in this rather arcane and highly controversial subject, there is a learned treatise on the subject on the *napoleon.org* website, and several books including *Napoléon* (1963) by Felix Markham, which has a whole appendix on the subject, which itself makes reference to E de Veauce's *L'Affaire du Masque de Napoléon* (1957).

Antommarchi signed bronze death mask, 1833

THE FAN CLUB

'Greatness be nothing unless it be lasting'

 LTHOUGH NOTHING IS forever, it is probable that the legend of Napoléon Bonaparte will survive a great deal longer than most. This is not just because of his meteoric rise to power, his glittering reign, and his spectacular fall. Nor is it because of his achievements as an exceptional military commander, and the endurance of his Civil Code. Nor is it because of the extraordinarily theatrical pageant that he devised and directed, and the survival of many of the buildings and artefacts of that imperial 'theatre'.

To varying degrees, some if not all of these attributes can be ascribed to legendary leaders from Moses to Margaret Thatcher and Herod to Hitler. Where Napoléon seems to trump all of them is with his 'fan club'. This started in his lifetime and endures to the present day in the form of private collectors, institutional collections and political imitators. Many of these – particularly the museums – have already been covered in earlier pages, but some of the individual collectors and a brace of the most notorious imitators are the subject of this chapter.

Napoléon in Milan, 1797

CONTEMPORARY COLLECTORS

By no means the most prolific of the individual collectors, but arguably one of the most important, was His Royal Highness Prince George August Frederick, Prince of Wales, later The Prince Regent and, for the last ten years of his life, His Majesty King George IV. 'Prinny', as George was both affectionately and derisorily known, was a complex character about whom many words have been written. Among his key characteristics were his material acquisitiveness, extravagant

opposite
King George IV

Prinny's Napoléonic desk

and vainglorious style, military delusions, his royal status, and an enthusiasm for the French First Empire.

At first sight, this enthusiasm for the First Empire is strange, given that for much of the time that the Imperial Impresario dominated the world's stage, Prinny was the nominal leader of one of the Emperor's most enduring enemies. He was also a genuine supporter of the exiled Bourbons, and the self-deluded 'vanquisher' of his hero. Nevertheless, he was a discerning collector of Napoléonica and aspired not only to rival the magnificence of the French imperial Court, but to exceed it. Thomas Moore, writing in his *Memoirs*, published in 1853, quotes his friend Prinny as stating on 24th October 1811 that it was his intention to 'quite eclipse Napoléon'. This may have been an inverted case of loving the sinner while loathing the sin.

In practice, however, this ambition did not lead the Prince to instruct his Paris-based agent (and former confectioner), François Benois, to acquire specifically First Empire furniture, although the ex-*pâtissier* did acquire for him a huge desk by the Jacob Frères, in the belief that it had belonged to the Emperor, and at a cost of £207 (2020: £20,459). However, the main focus of Benois's purchases was furniture of the period of Louis XVI, and the work of Jean-Henri Riesener in particular, although he did purchase some items in silver-gilt and a *nécessaire de voyage*, all of which had a Napoléonic provenance.

Carlton House, London, *c.* 1819

That said, the French First Empire style had a considerable influence on the only slightly less extravagant, British-made Regency style, as executed by the architects John Nash and Thomas Hope amongst others. This was popularised by The Prince Regent first at Carlton House and later at the remodelled Buckingham Palace. The royal stylist was also a willing recipient of gifts of Napoléonica, including the magnificent *Table of the Great Commanders of Antiquity*, commissioned by Napoléon in 1806, and given to Prinny by a grateful Louis XVIII. This table featured prominently in the Prince's future portraits.

In parenthesis, it is worth noting that Prinny's brother, the staunchly Whig Prince Augustus Frederick, Duke of Sussex, was not only a vociferous supporter of Napoléon, particularly during the St Helena exile, but was also a collector of Napoléonica. However, at the death of the impoverished Duke in 1843, his collection was sold at auction by Christie's; buyers at the sale included Madame Tussaud and Mr John Davis Sainsbury.

The Prince Regent's royal contemporary and military ally, King Frederick William III of Prussia, was another willing royal recipient of his defeated foe's memorabilia, including Napoléon's hat, sword, Orders and decorations, but was less obviously influenced by the French First Empire. This was in stark contrast to Tsar Alexander I of Russia, whose personal relationship with Napoléon lurched from one emotional extreme to another. Nevertheless, he embraced the new French style not only in the decoration and furnishing of his palaces (thereby creating the Russian Empire style) but also in the design of public buildings and monuments.

The most notable of these to be erected in Saint Petersburg during Alexander's reign were the General Staff Building and the Narva Triumphal Arch. The former was built opposite the Winter Palace, and consists of a huge, bow-shaped neo-classical office block designed by the Italian architect, Carlo Rossi.

Table of the Great Commanders

Royal Collection Trust © Her Majesty Queen Elizabeth II 2021

from the left

The Duke of Sussex (1773–1843); King Frederick William III of Prussia (1770–1840); Tsar Alexander I of Russia (1777–1825)

Madame Tussaud

Sir John Soane (1753–1837)

Erected to commemorate Napoléon's defeat in Russia in 1812, it features, at its centre, a triumphal triple arch, the first of which is topped by a group of statues representing Victory.

The Narva Triumphal Arch was originally erected in wood to commemorate Napoléon's second defeat by the Russians in 1814. The design by Giacomo Quarenghi was based on the Arc de Triomphe du Carrousel in Paris. It was replaced in between 1827 and 1834 with a stone version designed by Vasily Stasov.

* * *

Prominent among the other contemporary, but non-royal, members of the fan club were the previously mentioned showmen. First, Madame Tussaud, and her sons, Francis and Joseph, who assembled one of the most impressive collections of Napoléonica in England, including many fine portraits and a death bed *tableau* of the Emperor that was viewed with approval by the 1st Duke of Wellington. Again in parenthesis, the Iron Duke was no fan of Napoléon, but nonetheless had a substantial collection of Napoléonica, including the aforementioned nude marble statue of Napoléon as *Mars the Peacemaker* by Canova. The statue was rejected by the Emperor in 1811, and hidden from public view on his command. It was presented as a gift to his nemesis in 1816 by the British government, which had purchased it from Louis XVIII. Wellington also had a large collection of Napoléonic militaria; Napoléon's Egyptian Service of china, made to commemorate the Egyptian Campaign; and some marble columns with an imperial provenance. Bought in Paris and intended for the never-built Waterloo Palace, they now surround the swimming pool at Stratfield Saye, Wellington's house in Hampshire.

The second of the showmen in the fan club was William Bullock, although he dispersed his collection at a very considerable profit within four years of its acquisition. Then there was Sir John Soane, the architect and founder of the eponymous museum in Lincoln's Inn Fields, albeit that he was rather more of a fan than a collector. That said, in addition to the mourning ring with a lock of the Emperor's hair, recently reacquired by the museum, Soane bought two small portraits, one of a young Napoléon and the other of the over-weight 'Corsican Monster', as well as two bronzes and a plaster bust of the Emperor. He also acquired what was thought at the time to be Napoléon's Turkish silver pistol, allegedly given to the Emperor by Tsar Alexander I. Tim Knox, former Director of the Sir John Soane's Museum and now Director of the Royal Collection Trust adds:

'There is a strange story of how the pistol was acquired. An old lady was apprehended by the police trying to sell it on the streets, as it was suspected stolen. This was reported in the local newspaper, and Soane offered to buy it. In fact, it was an Albanian gun with an elaborate, fictitious, inscription.'

Whatever its true provenance, the pistol was stolen from the museum in 1969. To these items Soane added an assortment of Napoléonic commemorative medallions, and some fifty books; the latter included a special edition of Percier and Fontaine's treatise on palaces and grand houses with hand-coloured illustrations, which had been presented to their patroness, Joséphine.

Soane's enthusiasm for Napoléon, as with his interest in the eighteenth-century Indian ruler, Tipu Sultan, and other leaders, was partly driven by his fascination with the hubristic nature of the Emperor's rise and fall. However, it probably had more to do with his hero's embellishment of central Paris, particularly the grand processional route from the Arc de Triomphe to the Tuileries, and the unrealised plans for the proposed imperial palace and office complex on the hill at Chaillot. Soane had his own grandiose plans for London, which were never realised. Further evidence as to what really motivated Soane's interest in Napoléon, is provided by his refusal in 1835 to buy for £6,000 (2020: £780,000) another extensive Napoléonica collection.

This belonged to the Napoléon fan and collector, John Davis Sainsbury. Born in 1793, Sainsbury started his working life as a Smithfield coal merchant. However, from 1823 he had an office in Salisbury Square, Fleet Street, London, where he established himself as a literary, clerical and scholastic agent, as well as being a music and book seller who published the ground-breaking *Dictionary of Music from the Earliest Ages to the Present Time* (Longman) in 1824. Sainsbury may also have been a cousin and forebear of the discerning and acquisitive grocers of the same name, who established their business in Drury Lane in 1869, and became the leading patrons of the arts in Britain in the twentieth century.

Back in the nineteenth century, the former-coal-merchant Sainsbury acquired his Napoléonica at various auctions from 1820 onwards including books belonging to Joséphine, bought in 1831 from the estate of her grandson, Prince Napoléon-Louis Bonaparte, son of Hortense de Beauharnais. In 1834, the year before his offer to Soane, he published a catalogue of the collection, presumably as a sales tool. Having failed to sell his Napoléonica to the architect, Sainsbury carried on collecting. His numerous acquisitions included buying a bust and a miniature of the Emperor from the Christie's sale of the Duke of Sussex's collection in June 1834, at which Madame Tussaud also bought several items. On 12th April 1843, Sainsbury put his collection on display in what he rather grandiloquently called the Napoléon Museum. This he established in rented space at the Egyptian Hall, Piccadilly, the former site of Bullock's Museum. Entry cost a shilling (2020: £6.50).

Sainsbury produced and published a later, expanded catalogue in 1843 as a museum guide (price: one shilling), and a deluxe 650-page illustrated, morocco leather-bound version in 1845. Both of these catalogues had the rather lengthy

Sketch of John Davis Sainsbury at the Napoléon Museum

title: *Catalogue of the Napoléon Museum or, Illustrated History of France, from Louis XIV to the end of the Reign and Death of the Emperor Napoléon: Collected during the last 25 Years by John Sainsbury*. From these records it appears that, like Soane's collection but unlike Tussaud's and Bullock's, Sainsbury had acquired only a few items that had actually belonged to Napoléon, other than autographed letters and documents. He was also, unlike Soane and Tussaud but like Bullock, not a long-term collector, for the lavish 1845 special-edition catalogue was almost certainly published, like its 1834 predecessor, to warm-up the market for the sale of the collection in that year.

According to the British Museum, the auction of the contents of the Napoléon Museum 'made little money' for Mr Sainsbury. So Madame Tussaud got bargains when she bought a bust of the Emperor by the Italian sculptor, Antonio Trentanove, and the *Apotheosis of Napoléon* by Louis-Jean-François Lagrenée. The latter, depicting Napoléon as a Roman Emperor, was described by Joseph Bonaparte as 'the most perfect likeness of the Emperor' he had ever seen; it should not to be confused with the work of the same name by Ingres, now in the Louvre. According to Christie's records, Sainsbury paid £500 (2020: £65,000) for it at the Sussex auction, but there is no record of the price it achieved in the Sainsbury sale.

The low prices achieved by the sale of the Napoléon Museum's collection was almost certainly because of the largely impersonal nature of the items on offer: the 1845 catalogue lists an Eagle finial of an unspecified Regiment of the Imperial Guard, and dozens of busts, statuettes and pictures of the Emperor, but about the only really personal items in the collection were a pair of Napoléon's white silk stockings worn on St Helena, with a certificate to that effect.

Sainsbury was still in financial difficulties when he was taken to Court by an auction house over a loan (*Chinnock v. Sainsbury*) in 1860. During the hearing, Sainsbury claimed that he had spent over £40,000 (2020: £5 million) on collecting since 1820, which if true had given him a poor return on his enormous investment. The moral of the story is that, for a guaranteed increase in value, buy Boney's underwear.

*   *   *

6th Duke of Devonshire
(1790–1858)

As well as the monarchs and the showmen, the Imperial Impresario enjoyed during his lifetime a select but distinguished fan club in the British aristocracy, of whom the leading enthusiast was the unmarried William George Spencer Cavendish, 6th Duke of Devonshire, known as the 'Bachelor Duke'. He was responsible for the significant enlargement of Chatsworth House in Derbyshire; the installation there of a vast iron and glass greenhouse designed by Joseph Paxton; and the acquisition of a small but important collection of Napoléonic statues for his newly constructed Sculpture Gallery.

At the heart of this collection is the huge marble bust of the Emperor by the Duke's friend, Antonio Canova. This was actually acquired by Anne, Marchioness of Abercorn after Canova death in 1822, and bequeathed to the 6th Duke in her Will when she died in 1827. As impressive artistically, is the sculptor's iconic statue of a seated Madame Mère, and a similar composition depicting Napoléon's sister, Pauline Borghese, by the Rome-based Scottish sculptor, Thomas Campbell. In this representation, unlike Canova's *Venus Victrix* in which Pauline is completely bare breasted, she has only her left one on display. Smaller busts by Canova of the two ladies, with whom the Duke had become friendly after 1815, were acquired by him during their lifetime, along with some Napoléonic portraits.

Another British Duke with a collection of Napoléonica was that of Alexander Hamilton, 10th Duke of Hamilton. Like Devonshire, he was a Whig and (like most Whigs) an admirer of the Emperor. In 1811, at the very height of the Anglo-French hostilities and in defiance of the *zeitgeist*, he took the extraordinary decision to commission Jacques-Louis David to paint a full-length portrait of his hero at a cost of £1,000 (2020: £82,600). On its delivery the following year,

below, from left
Madame Mère by Canova, Chatsworth House, Derbyshire; *Pauline Borghese*, Chatsworth House, Derbyshire; *Napoléon* by Canova, Chatsworth House, Derbyshire

10th Duke of Hamilton (1767–1852)

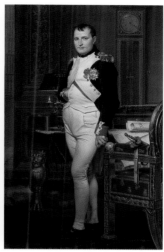

The Emperor Napoléon in his Study at the Tuileries hung first in the Billiard Room and then in the Dining Room at the aptly-named Hamilton Palace in South Lanarkshire. However, it was sold at auction in 1882 to help pay-down the considerable, accumulated ducal debts of the 11th and 12th Dukes, at which time it was bought by Archibald Primrose, 5th Earl of Rosebery. It remained in his family's collection, until it was purchased in 1954 by the Samuel H. Kress Foundation which deposited in the National Gallery of Art in Washington, DC, USA, where it still hangs.

Other items of Hamilton-owned Napoléonica to go under the hammer in the 1882 sale were a bust of the Emperor by Bertel Thorvaldsen, similar to the one lost in the Madame Tussaud's fire, which sold to J. B. Greenshields of Kerse, Lanarkshire, for £640 (2020: £78,733) and is now believed to be in the Thorvaldsen Museum in Copenhagen, Denmark; and Pauline Borghese's *nécessaire de voyage* by Biennais, bequeathed to the 10th Duke in her Will and now in the National Museums of Scotland. Not disposed of in the 1882 sale was the Emperor's silver-gilt tea service, also by Biennais, which had been commissioned for his marriage to Marie Louise in 1810 and was purchased by the 10th Duke in 1830 for F17,000 (2020: c. £50,000). The extensive service was held in two chests: the first was sold to the French government in 1919 and is now in the Louvre Museum, and the second was sold to the National Museums of Scotland in 1976.

As a footnote to the Hamilton collection, and in a neat piece of symmetry, the 10th Duke was married to Susan Beckford, daughter of the notoriously reclusive millionaire, William Beckford, who built the Gothic Revival Fonthill Abbey. His only guests there were Napoléon's nautical nemesis, Vice Admiral of the White

above, from left
Hamilton Palace, Lanarkshire;
Napoléon in his Study at the
Tuileries

Susan Beckford, Duchess
of Hamilton (1786 –1859)

Viscount Nelson, the Admiral's mistress, Emma, Lady Hamilton, and her husband, the diplomat and antiquarian, Sir William Hamilton. This notorious *menage* visited the Abbey on the evening of 23rd March 1801 for dinner, but actually stayed in Beckford's Palladian mansion, Fonthill Splendens. Continuing the marital and historical symmetry, William, 11th Duke of Hamilton, married Prinzessin Marie-Amelie of Baden, the daughter of Napoléon's adopted daughter, Stéphanie de Beauharnais. This saga of Napoléonic symmetry was completed by the 11th Duke's grandson, who was Prince Louis II of Monaco.

Further down the aristocratic pecking order was Arthur George Onslow, 3rd Earl of Onslow, who amassed a considerable collection of Napoléonica. This included commissioning *Napoléon Crossing the Alps* from Paul Delaroche in 1848, as a more realistic depiction of the actual event than Jacques-Louis David's absurdly heroic misrepresentation of the facts. Delaroche studied the accounts of the First Consul's crossing of the Saint Bernard Pass in 1800, and possibly visited the site to get first-hand knowledge of the landscape. The mountain guide who had accompanied the future Emperor at the time was long since dead, but his account was well known, as was Napoléon's own record of the event in his memoirs. The First Consul had actually, as Delaroche depicts, crossed the Saint Bernard, not in a billowing cloak seated on a pale grey Arab as shown by David, but hunched in a greatcoat on a borrowed mule with a local guide by his side. The original painting is now in the Walker Art Gallery, Liverpool.

Henry Vassal-Fox, the 3rd Baron Holland and his wife, Elizabeth, were also fervent fans of Napoléon who, unlike their contemporaries described above, had actually met the First Consul and Joséphine in Paris in 1802. During the Emperor's

below, from left
Lord Holland (1773-1840);
Lady Holland (1771-1845);
Bust of Napoléon at Holland
House, London

exile on Elba, Lady Holland sent him newspapers and periodicals. In 1815, she commissioned a bust of the Napoléon from Canova, for the garden at Holland House in London. Later, while her husband objected in the House of Lords to Napoléon's exile in the South Atlantic, she sent Napoléon more than 1,000 books, crates of his beloved (and possibly deadly) Eau de Cologne, journals, an ice-making machine, and food parcels. In gratitude, Napoléon bequeathed her a gold snuff box, inset on the lid with an agate cameo of Bacchus on a goat, presented to him by Pope Pius VI. Lady Holland in turn bequeathed it to the British Museum on her death in 1845.

The last of the aristocratic collectors to be considered here is Charles Stuart, who from 1828 was the 1st (and last) Baron Stuart de Rothesay. Stuart was the grandson of an Earl and the great-grandson of a Duke, but entered the British diplomatic service in 1801 as plain Mr Charles Stuart. He served first as Secretary of the British Legation at Vienna, then Secretary of the Embassy at St Petersburg. Between 1808 and 1810, he was a spy in French-occupied Spain, later making himself indispensable to Wellington as British Minister at Lisbon from 1810 to 1814. His next diplomatic appointments were successively as Minister at The Hague, and then British Minister to Louis XVIII for The Hundred Days, during which he attended the Duchess of Richmond's Ball in Brussels, three days before the Battle of Waterloo. After the Emperor's second Abdication, Sir Charles (as he had become in 1812) remained in Paris as the British Minister until 1824, and served a second term there between 1828 and 1831. His service as a diplomat ended in 1844, when he retired for reasons of ill health as the British Ambassador in Saint Petersburg.

Lord Stuart de Rothesay
(1779–1845)

Although a fervent supporter of the Bourbon Restoration, Stuart befriended several Bonapartes. While at the British Embassy in Paris, he amassed a substantial collection of First Empire furniture, ceramics, metalwork, books and other decorative items. The core of this collection had belonged to Marshal Ney, and was sold in 1817 to Sir Charles by the Marshal's widow from the Hôtel de Saisseval. This was Ney's house in Paris, which Napoléon had helped him to buy in 1805, and was furnished lavishly in the First Empire style. The contents of the Hôtel de Saisseval were installed by Sir Charles at the British Embassy in Paris (the Hôtel de Charôst, the former residence of Pauline Borghese) and then at Highcliffe Castle, his newly rebuilt Gothic Revival home in Dorset.

On the death of his second wife in 1867, Lord Stuart de Rothesay's First Empire collection was inherited by his younger daughter, Louisa Beresford, Marchioness of Waterford, who retained Highcliffe Castle and its contents. She in turn left the house and its collection to her distant cousin, Major General Edward Stuart Wortley. When his younger daughter Elizabeth (known as Bettine)

Highcliffe Castle, Dorset

Highcliffe Castle interior

Part of the Hôtel de Saisseval
suite by Jacob-Desmalter

married Montagu Bertie, 8th Earl of Abingdon, in 1928, he bought the castle and
its contents from his father-in-law. Twenty-one years later the Abingdons sold
Highcliffe and most of its contents, while retaining a number of Marshal Ney's
pieces.

After her husband's death in 1963, Lady Abingdon lived for much of the time
with her close friends, Mr and Mrs Tahu Hole, to whom she bequeathed all her
personal possessions on her death in 1978. Tahu Hole died in 1985, and a year
later his widow approached the Victoria and Albert Museum and offered the
collection as a bequest. When Joyce Hole died in December 1986, and in
accordance with her Will, the museum chose those items that it wished to add to
its collections; other items in the bequest were sold to benefit the museum, and
the proceeds were added to the funds bequeathed.

Included in the items retained by the V&A was a set of ormolu-mounted
mahogany furniture made for the Hôtel de Saisseval by the imperial cabinet
maker, François-Honoré-Georges Jacob-Desmalter. Upholstered in brocaded

blue silk, the suite was originally installed in the Petit Salon at the Paris mansion and consisted of two large bergères, two smaller bergères, two other bergères, two fauteuils, four side chairs, two X-framed tables and one tabouret de pied. At auction today, and with the Ney provenance, this suite would probably be worth many times more than its value of F900 (2020: £2,493) in 1815.

LATER COLLECTORS

Some of the later, non-contemporary private collectors of Napoléonica had a familial connection to the Emperor or the extended Imperial Family, which may have driven their enthusiasm. Chief amongst these was Prince Louis II of Monaco, who spent much of his youth serving in the French Foreign Legion and the French Army during the First World War. He started collecting Napoléonica in 1922, when he ascended the serene and velvet-covered bench of his tiny Mediterranean principality.

Prince Louis II of Monaco

Rather more closely connected to the Bonapartes by blood than the Monegasque ruler was Comte Giuseppe Napoléone Primoli, whose mother was born Charlotte (Carlotta) Bonaparte. She was a great niece of Napoléon on both sides of her family: her father was Charles Lucien Bonaparte, 2nd Prince de Canino and Musignano, the son of the Emperor's brother, Lucien; and her mother was Zénaïde Laetitia Julie Bonaparte, daughter of Napoléon's brother, Joseph.

Principally known in his lifetime as a photographer, Primoli was a friend of some of the leading writers of his day, including Guy de Maupassant and Alexander Dumas *fils*. He was also an avid collector of books, prints, Napoléonica of every description, and documents linking the Bonaparte family and Rome. These he amassed at the Palazzo Primoli, his family's house in the Eternal City.

On his death in 1927, the Count left the palazzo, his collection of photographs and his books to the Fondazione Primoli, and his Napoléonica to the Museo Napoléonico, which has ever since occupied the ground floor of his house. There, in a sequence of beautifully conserved rooms, are displayed documents, paintings, costumes, sculpture, furniture and *objets d'art* featuring the First Empire (Rooms I and II), the Second Empire (Room III), the King of Rome (Room IV), the Roman Republic (Room V), Pauline Bonaparte (Room VI), The Kingdom of Naples (Room VII), Napoléon himself (Room VIII), Charlotte and Zénaïde Bonaparte (Room IX), Lucien Bonaparte (Room X), The Bonapartes in Rome (Room XI), Giuseppe Primoli and his great aunt, Matilde Bonaparte (Room XII). These treasures can be viewed on the museum's extraordinarily well-presented virtual tour. This is accessed by logging on to *www.tourvirtuale.museonapoléonico.it*.

A later collection that has not survived intact was that of the Danish-born

Comte Primoli (1851–1925)

right
Queen Alexandra, when
Princess of Wales (1844–1925);
Napoléonic Room at
Marlborough House
Royal Collection Trust © Her Majesty
Queen Elizabeth II 2021

Teapot by Biennais
Royal Collection Trust © Her Majesty
Queen Elizabeth II 2021

Tea caddy by Biennais
Royal Collection Trust © Her Majesty
Queen Elizabeth II 2021

British Queen Alexandra, which she assembled as Princess of Wales and displayed in a room at Marlborough House in London. Packed in typical Edwardian style, according to Kathryn Jones, Senior Curator of Decorative Arts for the Royal Collect Trust) 'this room was filled with paintings, prints, miniatures, statuettes, busts and other images of Napoléon, within a setting of First Empire furniture and silk-lined walls bearing wreaths in the manner of Percier and Fontaine'. Although photographs of the room still exist in the Royal Collection, no inventory of Alexandra's collection was ever made and only a few items remain in the Royal Collection. These include First Empire and First Empire-revival furniture, now in the Empire Room at Buckingham Palace; a lock of the Emperor's hair; and a silver-gilt teapot and caddy by Biennais, part of yet another imperial *nécessaire de voyage*.

The reason for this post-Regency revival of British royal interest in Napoléon is not clear. Neither Queen Victoria or her husband, Prince Albert of Saxe-Coburg-Gotha, were blood relations, although she famously succumbed to the charms of Napoléon III. During a State Visit to Paris in 1855, Victoria visited the imperial tomb at Les Invalides, noting in her diary 'I stood on the arm of Napoléon III, before the coffin of his Uncle, our bitterest foe!' She also acquired a copy of the painting by Delaroche of *Napoléon Crossing the Alps*, to which she added *Napoléon in Exile on St Helen* [*sic*].

Unlike the Swedish Royal Family, the Danish Royal House of Schleswig-Holstein-Sonderburg-Glücksburg, from which Queen Alexandra sprang, also had no prior blood connections to the Bonapartes or to the Empress Joséphine's de Beauharnais children. That said, Alexandra's nephew, Prince George of

from left

Prince George of Greece
and Denmark (1869–1957);
Princess George of Greece and
Denmark, née Marie Bonaparte
(1882–1962); Queen Mary
(1867–1953)]

Cameo portrait ring

Royal Collection Trust © Her Majesty
Queen Elizabeth II 2021

Greece and Denmark, was married to Marie Bonaparte, a great-granddaughter of Napoléon's brother, Lucien, and a cousin of Comte Giuseppe Primoli. Unfortunately for the authors' quest for historical symmetry, Marie and George were not married until 1907, a good five years *after* Alexandra had moved reluctantly from Marlborough House to Buckingham Palace. So, prior to 1907, there was no familial connection to Napoléon in the British Royal Family.

Nor was there any obvious connection to Queen Mary, the wife of Queen Alexandra's son, King George VI. She was an avid collector of antiques, including Napoléonica, but had no ties of blood to the Emperor beyond that of her husband's cousin-by-marriage, Marie Bonaparte. Nonetheless, she acquired for the Royal Collection a gold ring set with an agate cameo portrait in profile of Napoléon; and a bloodstone snuff box with gold mounts, said to have belonged to Pauline Borghese and containing a lock of her hair. At another Hamilton sale in 1934, she bought a pair of toast racks, a tea urn, a tea pot, a milk jug, a ewer, a tazza and several other items from a silver-gilt tea service by Henri Auguste, that had belonged to Stéphanie de Beauharnais. A silver-gilt beaker from one of the Emperor's *nécessaires de voyage* by Biennais, also acquired in 1934 but not at the Hamilton sale, and other silver-gilt items, probably from a *nécessaire* with a Napoléonic provenance, joined her collection. Most of these items were intended by Queen Mary to be displayed in the Grand Vestibule at Windsor Castle, alongside the Napoléonica acquired by The Prince Regent.

Away from the ranks of monarchy and the old aristocracy (and passing over Isabella Stewart Gardner, Count Demidov, Bernard Ledoux, the Baghot family and other collections referenced in earlier chapters) are two further private-turned-public collections assembled by Napoléon's later fans.

The first was that amassed by the Edwardian soap magnate and noted Napoléonist, William Lever, 1st Viscount Leverhulme, who was known during his lifetime

Ewer by Henri Auguste

Royal Collection Trust © Her Majesty
Queen Elizabeth II 2021

above, from left
1st Viscount Leverhulme (1851–1925), 'The Napoléon of Soap';
Room 9, Lady Lever Art Gallery

(appropriately given his enthusiasm for the Emperor) as the 'Napoléon of Soap'. His collection of First Empire furniture and decorative items are on display in the Napoléon Room (Room 9) at the Lady Lever Art Gallery, Port Sunlight, now part of the National Museums of Liverpool. However, none of the items on display belonged to Napoléon himself, although some may have a link to the Emperor's half-uncle, Cardinal Joseph Fesch, or to Joséphine's house, Malmaison. According to the museum, most of the collection was made during the Second French Empire, including both the death masks of Napoléon on display.

Perhaps the most unlikely of all the private collections-turned-public institutions, is to be found in the communist state of Cuba at the Museo Napoléonico. It is housed in Villa Fiorentina, a former private house in San Miguel Street, Havana, built in the 1920s in the Florentine Renaissance style by Evilio Govantes and Félix Cabarrocas for the Italian-Cuban pre-Castro-era revolutionary politician, author and newspaper-owner, Orestes Ferrera.

The collection consists of 8,000 items, dating from the French Revolution to the Second French Empire, largely bought at auction in the first half of the twentieth century by Julio Lobo, a Venezuelan financier and art connoisseur, who was married to a Cuban aristocrat. At the time of the Cuban Revolution of 1959, Lobo was reputed to be the richest and most powerful sugar trader in the world, with a fortune that today would be worth US$1.8 billion.

In the wake of Fidel Castro's coup, both Lobo and Ferrera fled Cuba (the former to Madrid and the latter to Rome), leaving all their tangible assets behind. The house was confiscated and the collection nationalised in 1960. Although Lobo and Ferrera undoubtedly knew each other, it was the revolutionary government that brought their properties together and established the museum in 1961. Coincidentally, this was in the same year as the failed counter-revolution, known as the Bay of Pigs Invasion, which was followed the next year by the Cuban Missile Crisis. As a direct result of these events, for the next forty years Cuba was, in effect, a pariah state and the Napoléon Museum suffered accordingly.

A rare British visitor to the museum in 2004 reported that the Lobo collection was then a sad and neglected display, largely made up of, in his expert opinion, 'copies or reproduction items, many of them really nasty', despite having been valued in 1986 at US$8 million (2020: c. £24 million). In 2009 the museum closed for a complete renovation, which included rearranging the collection in chronological order. It was reopened in March 2011 by Princesse Alix Bonaparte, the widow of Prince Louis Napoléon (known to Bonapartists as Napoléon VI), who presented the museum with an imperial china service. This was added – according to the description of the museum in the public domain – to the furniture by Jacob-Desmalter; bronzes by Thomire, including an eighteen-branch chandelier designed by Percier that was made for Joséphine's house in the Rue de la Victoire and moved with her to Malmaison; paintings of the Emperor and the Imperial Family by Gérard, Lefevre, Gros and others; porcelain, sculptures, militaria, coins, personal items belonging to Napoléon and his entourage; and books, engravings and autographed letters.

Julio Lobo (1898–1983)

Whether or not these items are genuine or reproduction, the centrepiece of the museum's collection is without doubt a copy. This is a bronze subscription edition of Dr Antommarchi' death mask of the Emperor, made in 1833 by L. Richard and E. Quesnel of Paris, and later bought at auction. In yet another piece of historical symmetry, Dr Antommarchi travelled to Cuba in 1837 to study yellow fever, and died there of the disease on the 3rd April 1838.

THE IMITATORS

If imitation is the sincerest form of flattery, then two notorious twentieth-century figures must stand out, not only as high-profile fans of Napoléon, but also as sincere flatters. The first is Adolf Hitler, the teetotal, vegetarian, totally unscrupulous and notoriously flatulent dictator of Germany from 1934-1945, who in 1940 ordered the transfer of the King of Rome's remains from Vienna to lie with his father in Les Invalides in Paris. More memorably, he adopted two Napoléonic icons for his murderous regime, itself characterised by significantly more military theatricality than the First Empire.

The first was the eagle-and-swastika topped standards, deliberately reminiscent of imperial Eagles; and second was the so-called Hitler or *Sieg Heil* salute, self-evidently modelled on Napoléon's Roman *adlocutio* salute, as depicted by Jacques-

above, from left
Napoléon's *adlocutio;*
Nazi Party standards;

Louis David in his painting of the *Distribution of Eagle Standards* in 1840. Like Napoléon, Hitler is still remembered (albeit with horror), and he too retains a residual fan club, membership of which – unlike Napoléon enthusiasts – is illegal in most civilised countries.

Much less well remembered than the flatulent Führer, despite having been in power more recently, is Jean-Bédel Bokassa, the self-styled Emperor of the so-called Central African Empire from 1976 to 1979. Bokassa started his adult life by joining the ranks of a French colonial Regiment in 1939, transferring to the Free French Forces in 1941 and remaining in the French Army after the war, during which time he was commissioned and awarded both the *Légion d'honneur* and the *Croix de Guerre* for his wartime service.

In 1962, Bokassa transferred to the nascent Central African Armed Forces (CAAF) of the newly independent republic as a Lieutenant Colonel. Within a year, he was Commander-in-Chief of the 500-strong CAAF, and in 1965 he organised a military *coup d'État* that toppled President David Dacko. In a move

reminiscent of the aftermath of the French Brumaire coup of 1799, Bokassa retained the republic's democratic name, but tore up the constitution and abolished the National Assembly, which he described as 'a lifeless organ no longer representing the people.' In a further echo of the events that led to the establishment of the First Empire, in 1969 Bokassa foiled a plot to unseat him that was led by his long-term colleague, Alexandre Banza. The failed coup leader was then murdered by Bokassa in circumstances reported by *Le Monde*:

above and top
Jean-Bedel, Emperor
Bokassa I (1921–1996)

> 'Two versions concerning the end circumstances of his death differ on one minor detail. Did Bokassa tie him to a pillar before personally carving him with a knife that he had previously used for stirring his coffee in the gold-and-midnight blue Sèvres coffee set, or was the murder committed on the cabinet table with the help of other persons? Late that afternoon, soldiers dragged a still identifiable corpse, with the spinal column smashed, from barrack to barrack to serve as an example.'

At least the Louis Antoine de Bourbon, Duc d'Enghien, was merely shot on the orders of Napoléon in 1804.

However, unlike the rapid evolution of the French Consulate into the First Empire, it was a further eight years before Bokassa proclaimed himself Emperor Bokassa I of the newly-designated Central African Empire, following which he staged a lavish sub-Saharan Coronation. This extravagant display was modelled on Napoléon's Coronation of 1804, albeit that it was held in a new, Yugoslav-built, sports stadium. Nevertheless, it involved the commissioning from French suppliers of numerous portraits, elaborate Court uniforms and Coronation robes, two crowns and other imperial regalia, costing at today's value £24.5 million. A gilded bronze throne in the shape of an eagle, weighing two tons and costing £12 million, two imperial carriages and harnesses (one in pink and the other in pale blue), 24,000 bottles of champagne, and sixty new Mercedes limousines were also delivered. The cars were intended as the local transport for the Pope and other invited Heads of State, all of whom – with the exception of the Grand Duc de Liechtenstein – declined to attend. The total cost of this farcical extravaganza at today's values was £108 million, a sum that represented at the time a third of the country's GDP, although it was significantly less than the £500 million spent on the 2,500th anniversary celebrations of the Achaemenid Empire, staged in 1971 at Persepolis by Shah Mohammad Reza Pahlavi of the oil-rich Iran; but then the Shah could afford such displays – at least for as long as he remained on the Peacock Throne.

Just over two years after Bokassa's Coronation in 1977, in the wake of food riots, massacres and the deliberate killing of a hundred children for refusing to

Persepolis, 1971

wear the State-approved school uniform, the self-styled Emperor, who at the time was on a State Visit to the equally repellent Libyan regime of Colonel Gaddafi, was overthrown in a French-supported coup in September 1979. With the reinstatement of his predecessor in his absence, and the end of the Central African Empire, the deposed Emperor fled to Ivory Coast where he stayed for four years before moving, with the benefit of political asylum and a French Army pension, to his château in France.

In October 1986, Bokassa returned unexpectedly to his former empire and was immediately arrested and charged with multiple counts of treason, murder, illegal use of property, assault and battery, embezzlement, and cannibalism. He was convicted on all but the last charge and sentenced to death. This was almost immediately commuted to life imprisonment in solitary confinement, later reduced to twenty years. He actually served only a relatively short time in prison and was released under an amnesty in 1993. The increasingly demented Bokassa spent the remainder of his life in the Central African Republic, where he declared himself to be the 13th Apostle and to have had regular meetings with the Pope. He died of a heart attack at the age of seventy-five in 1996, surrounded by some of his seventeen wives and fifty children.

Somewhat in the manner of Napoléon, but with considerably less justification, Bokassa was 'rehabilitated' by a Presidential Decree in 2010, in which he was described as a patriot and 'a son of the nation, recognised by all as a great builder'. Outside the Central African Republic, Emperor Bokassa I is now an almost entirely forgotten figure, and certainly one without a fan club. This is unlike Napoléon, who used *his* second exile to ensure his posthumous reputation and a burgeoning army of fans.

CHAPTER TEN

THE FINAL CURTAIN

'My downfall raises me to infinite heights'

NLIKE HIS FIRST EXILE on Elba, where he reigned as Emperor over the small Mediterranean island with a cut-down Household and a tiny army consisting largely of units of the Imperial Guard, on St Helena Napoléon had no such privileges. Nonetheless, for a political prisoner he enjoyed a degree of freedom not granted to others in a similar position. Not for the imperial exile a barren prison cell in a dank fortress. Instead, after a three-month delay, he settled into Longwood House, a substantial, mist-shrouded, rat-infested barn-turned-bungalow on the sub-tropical island of St Helena, initially with a staff of forty-two which was later reduced to twenty-six. Other comforts included a tame capuchin monkey, and large quantities of baggage, carrying a selection of his linen, uniforms, china, glass and silver, all of which became extremely collectable.

Actually, this was not a fate that befell the monkey after its master's death, for it was brought back to England by Captain Thompson RN on the last voyage of the storeship, HMS *Abundance*. It then passed into the ownership of a British artist, Stephen Taylor, who immortalised it in oils. On the ape's death, Taylor buried it in his garden in Winchester. If, instead, the monkey had been stuffed, it would today be a prized and valuable item of Napoléonica.

Once on St Helena, Napoléon was not confined to his quarters, but allowed to go where he wished on the island, providing he was accompanied by a British officer. It was his choice to confine himself largely to Longwood and its garden, where he was not required to have a military minder. The real cell walls and jailors were not Longwood and the British military garrison, but the waves of the South Atlantic. Nevertheless, St Helena was a prison to which Napoléon had been

Longwood House, St Helena

opposite

François-Joseph Sandmann's
Napoléon à Sainte-Hélène c.1820

Napoléon dictating to Las Cases

General Bertrand

Fanny Bertrand (1785–1836)

committed without trial to serve a whole-life sentence. This was not his preferred solution, which was exile to a country estate either in England or the United States. However, it was probably preferable, even in the light of his attempted suicide at Fontainebleau in April 1814, to the pragmatic solution of the Prussians and the returning Bourbons, who argued for Napoléon's summary execution.

* * *

In the six years from his final defeat in 1815 to his death in 1821 Napoléon adopted a routine on St Helena that varied little. In stark contrast to his former life, he rose late and usually breakfasted at ten o'clock. This was followed by time spent dictating his memoirs, followed by lunch, a stroll in the garden or a drive in his carriage, and then more dictation and conversations. Dinner was usually at seven o'clock and would be followed by one of the Ladies of the Household reading to him aloud, often a book from the Classics, then a few hands of cards and bed at midnight.

This concluding chapter is not, however, so much concerned with the facts of Napoléon's final exile, nor his eventual death – some of the events and the spin-offs of which have already been considered – but rather with the way that the imperial exile (and others) used his banishment to ensure his legacy... by writing it. As with the use of pale grey chargers, Churchill and Napoléon were at one on this subject, the former saying in 1948 '...leave the past to history, especially as I intend to write it', and the latter who declared that 'history is the agreed version of past events', and then used his time on St Helena to ensure that it was *his* version as dictated to Comte Emmanuel de Las Cases.

In fact, several versions emerged, for some of those who guarded him on St Helena or shared his exile also penned his and their own reminiscences of events up to 1821. Not so Napoléon's former private secretary, Louis Antoine Fauvelet de Bourrienne, whose vast *Memoirs of Napoléon Bonaparte* was published in 1830, and was for a long time regarded as the definitive account. However, he was sacked by the First Consul in 1802 and never again enjoyed close proximity to Napoléon: his post-1802 anecdotes are, therefore, second or third hand at best. So, who were the players in the final Scene of the last Act of the Imperial Impresario's drama, whose writings have ensured that Napoléon's own account of his life is the one that predominates? Some have already made their entrances.

Top of this cast list were the Bertrands. General Comte Henri-Gatien Bertrand was the former Grand Master of the Imperial Household, who loyally followed his master into his first exile and continued in that role on St Helena, albeit with a much-reduced staff to master. Bertrand's wife, Fanny, later become embroiled in the death mask controversy, but long before that she had hysterics and threatened to throw herself off HMS *Bellerophon* in Plymouth harbour, when Napoléon told her that he was being sent to the South Atlantic. Her behaviour was occasioned not by the news of the fallen Emperor's exile, but by her correct belief that her husband would accompany him and would demand that she did too. Fanny was only pacified when she was assured that the stay would be short. It wasn't.

General Bertrand later publish *Les Cahiers de Sainte-Hélène*, a key account of the period, in which he noted day-by-day Napoléon words, the tensions with the petty and vindictive British Governor, Lieutenant General Sir Hudson Lowe, and the tumultuous life of the small French community. As François Houdeck, the most recent editor of *Les Cahiers* states:

Sir Hudson Lowe (1769–1844)

> 'They are the very picture of the man who put them down on paper: straightforward, factual, respectful, scrupulous, and, at some very specific moments, full of admiration, loyalty and then humanity towards a fallen Emperor in the twilight of his life'.

Next on the cast list were the de Montholons. General Comte Charles de Montholon was a career soldier, whose rise to the top of his profession owed less to his military skills, which he shamelessly fabricated, than to his loyalty to the Emperor, having opposed surrender in 1814. De Montholon's wife, Albine-Hélène, had two previous husbands and two sons before she married Charles in 1812, although he was probably the boys' father. A third son was born in 1814. She accompanied her husband quite willingly to St Helena, where – as the resident slapper – she gave birth to two daughters, one of whom may have been fathered by Napoléon, and the other by an English officer, Lieutenant Basil Jackson, of whom more in a moment. The General seems to have been quite unperturbed by his wife's loose behaviour, because he had his own mistress on the island. In any event, Albine-Hélène left the island with her young children in July 1819, not because of her extra-marital activities but on health grounds. De Montholon stayed to the bitter end, and later published *Récits de la Captivité de l'Empereur Napoléon à Sainte-Hélène* in the 1840s, while in exile in England.

General de Montholon (1783–1853)

Comte Emmanuel de Las Cases was a minor aristocrat of the *ancien regime* and had been an officer in the Bourbon Navy. While in poverty-stricken exile in London during the French Revolution, he rebranded himself as an atlas-maker. Returning to France after the Peace of Amiens in 1802, he attached himself to the new regime, but it was not until 1810 that he was appointed a Court Chamberlain and auditor of the Conseil d'État. This brought him into Napoléon's immediate orbit, and gave him the opportunity to attach himself to those fleeing with the fallen Emperor to Rochefort in 1815. There, with General Gourgaud and as a

Albine de Montholon (1779–1848)

fluent English-speaker, he took responsibility for negotiating Napoléon's exile with the British authorities. He too sailed for St Helena, accompanied by his son, also called Emmanuel.

Much of Las Cases time *en route* to, and while on the island, was spent taking dictation from Napoléon, who seemed to prefer him to the other memorialists, and would annotate proofs in his own hand that had been prepared by Emmanuel *fils*. In the fractious and claustrophobic atmosphere of Longwood, this inevitably caused tensions. However, before the situation could deteriorate to the point of open enmity, Las Cases was expelled by Hudson Lowe in December 1816 and his notes were confiscated. This banishment was for allegedly trying to smuggle two letters written by the imperial exile off St Helena.

It was not until after Napoléon's death that Las Cases was able to retrieve his papers from the Colonial Office in September 1821. After consulting Dr O'Meara's 1822 memoir (see below), he embellished and padded out his own account which he published with enormous success as *Le Mémorial de Sainte-Hélène* in 1823. At the time and for many years afterwards, this book was regarded as Napoléon's auto-biography. More recently, however, historians have cast doubt on the veracity of much of the contents, particularly some of the ex-Emperor's observations and aphorisms, which are now attributed to Las Cases's epigrammatic skills. Mean-while, the book continues to enjoy the status of a quasi-autobiography, even if it is generally accepted that Bertrand's *Les Cahiers de Sainte-Hélène* is a more accurate, albeit a less stimulating read.

The unmarried General Baron Gaspard Gourgaud was thirty-two when he accompanied Napoléon to St Helena. He lasted there rather longer than Las Cases, but not without incident. It seems that he suffered from a significant socio-military chip on his shoulder arising from his relatively humble birth, de Mon-tholon's seniority in rank (Gourgaud was, at the time, only a General of Brigade), and several implied slights including (in his view) his unsatisfactory accom-modation ('a veritable cellar') at Longwood, and his place at Napoléon's dining table below that of de Montholon.

In fact, so bad did the friction between Gourgaud and de Montholon become that Gourgaud challenged his senior to a duel, which was only prevented by the intervention of the imperial exile himself. It was a situation that could not last, and on 14th March 1818 Gourgaud left the island with Sir Hudson Lowe's blessing. On his arrival in London, he reported to the Colonial Office where he accused Napoléon of feigning illness, with the complicity of Dr O'Meara, in order to get off the island, and stated that the doctor was principally responsible for smuggling Napoléon's letters to Europe. The ex-Emperor was not relocated, but O'Meara was sacked and returned to England.

General Gourgaud (1783–1852)

It remains unclear why Gourgaud went to St Helena in the first place. It may have been to pursue a debt of F50,000 (2020: £138,500), which he said was owed to him by the fallen Emperor. His constant and unsuccessful pestering of Napoléon for the debt, or a pension for his mother in lieu, apparently turned his master against him, to the delight of de Montholon and Las Cases, who disliked him in equal measure. It may also have been why he received nothing in Napoléon's Will. If money was his motivation, then it is surprising that Gourgaud never attempted to make anything from the secret journal which he kept from the time of his arrival on the island. His *Journal de Ste-Hélène* was not published until 1899, long after the General had died in 1852.

Joseph Archambault (1796–1874)

One further mystery about Gourgaud remains. Was he actually playing a part on St Helena and in London? Was he, in fact, Napoléon's secret accomplice and emissary to Bonapartists in Europe, tasked with plotting his master's rescue? The British authorities certainly came to that conclusion, having discovered that, while in London, he had written on behalf of Napoléon to his wife, Marie Louise, and the Emperors of Russia and Austria. When this treachery came to light in November 1818, Gourgaud was arrested and deported to Hamburg.

What followed gives further credence to the possibility that Gourgaud was not what he had seemed. On the orders of Napoléon, his stepson Prince Eugène de Beauharnais gave Gourgaud F12,000 (2020: £33,240). The General later became not only a member of the Bonapartist Party in France, but was also one of those who went to St Helena in 1840 to return the imperial exile's remains to Paris. Add to this his robust criticism of two biographies of Napoléon, one of which led to a duel, and his unsuccessful attempt to have his supposed-enemy, de Montholon, included in the 1840 *retour des cendres*, and it starts to look as though Gourgaud was indeed playing a double game from very early on.

Lower down the pecking order there are even more French memorialists to be found, although these do not include either Achille Archambault, Napoléon's head groom, or his deputy and brother, Joseph Archambault. The latter was a victim of British cost-cutting in October 1816, when Sir Hudson Lowe ordered Napoléon to reduce his staff. However, instead of returning to France, Joseph took ship to New York, in company with another of the dismissed servants, Theodore Rousseau. In 1861, at the advanced age of sixty-five, Joseph enlisted in the 2nd Pennsylvania Cavalry to fight in the American Civil War, rising to the rank of Major the following year.

Louis-Joseph-Narcisse Marchand, Napoléon's valet-in-exile remained with his master until the very end, for which he was ennobled as a Count, a title that was later confirmed by Napoléon III. Marchand penned a memoir of the period from 1811 to 1821, entitled: *In Napoléon's Shadow*. It was first published, in two

Louis Marchand (1791-1876)

Mameluke Ali (1788–1856)

volumes in 1952 and 1955, and only appeared in an English translation in 1998. As the editor of the English version, Procter Jones, states:

'This is the last of the significant Napoléonic manuscripts to be translated into English... [and] the fascinating chronology of the lives of these two men makes what he has to say most interesting. Marchand does not try to write history. He writes an engaging reminiscence of experiences in the Imperial presence... [His account of] the Russian campaign, the campaigns of Germany and France, Elba, the Hundred Days, culminating in Waterloo and Saint Helena ... [are] all laid out in a clear and orderly fashion, practically day-by-day. Rich though it is as a daily record, it also relives the stories Napoléon recounted of past events.'

Another account that only became available in English in the twentieth century was that of Ali (Louis-Étienne) Saint Denis, Napoléon's Mameluke bodyguard and second valet, who wrote his *Souvenirs du Mameluck Ali sur l'Empereur Napoléon*. The memoir, largely anecdotal in style, was written by Saint Denis once he had returned to France from St Helena. It was compiled purely from memory, as he kept no contemporaneous notes, and was published in French in 1826, although the first English translation only appeared in 1922.

The last of Napoléon's staff to keep and publish an account of the events on St Helena was Dr Francesco Antommarchi. His diary of the ex-Emperor's medical care provided him with the material for *The Last Moments of the Emperor Napoléon*, which he published in 1825, and in which he concluded that the former Master of

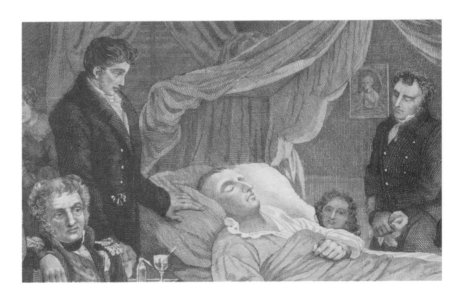

Dr Antommarchi (standing, with his hand on the pillow) at Napoléon's deathbed

Europe had died of stomach cancer. The book does not, however, shed any light on the stories of Napoléon's severed penis or the contested death mask.

Dr Barry O'Meara

* * *

Meanwhile, Napoléon's English jailors were also keeping their own accounts. Despite being encouraged by the British government to publish his own *ex post facto* account, Sir Hudson Lowe was not one of them. The principal memorialists were Dr Barry O'Meara, his successor Dr John Stokoe, Lieutenant Basil Jackson, and Betsy Balcombe.

O'Meara's first met Napoléon on HMS *Bellerophon*, while serving as the ship's surgeon. Possibly because the doctor spoke good Italian and passable French, the ex-Emperor, whose English was poor, requested that the Irishman accompany him in exile as his personal physician. On the seventy-two-day journey to St Helena the two men bonded. Once on the island, O'Meara quickly became not only a confidante but also a keen post-prandial audience for Napoléon, who proposed (doubtless as part of his mission to ensure that history was recorded in his own words) that the physician should keep a record of their conversations. When O'Meara somewhat naively asked why, Napoléon replied: 'It will make you a fortune, but please do not publish until after I am dead'. The result was an eighteen-hundred-page diary.

After considerable editing, but no deletion of his barbed views on Sir Hudson Lowe, in 1822 O'Meara published the diary in two-volumes as *Napoléon in Exile*,

Napoléon on board
HMS *Bellerophon*

Dr James Verling (1787–1858)

Dr John Stokoe (1775–1852)

or A Voice from St Helena. The book was an instant commercial success, as well as damning the Governor for posterity. The money and the revenge must have been some considerable consolation to O'Meara for the events between his recall from St Helena in 1818 and the book's publication. These included an attempt by the Admiralty to shut him up with the offer of the prestigious post of consultant surgeon to both the Greenwich and the Chelsea Royal Hospitals. The Irishman refused to stay silent and, two weeks later, was not only dismissed from the service but struck off the medical register and denied his pension. Undeterred by this ruthlessly unfair treatment, the resilient physician leveraged his extraction of the imperial molars by re-branding himself as a dentist, with premises on Edgeware Road in London. There, by way of an advertisement, he put one of the imperial teeth on display in the window along with a written endorsement of his skill at extractions. Three years later and, as Napoléon had predicted, with both fame and considerable wealth arising from his book, O'Meara abandoned dentistry and took to after dinner speaking, dying in 1836 from influenza. The tooth, which O'Meara left in his Will to Napoleon's brother, Prince Lucien Bonaparte, was the one lost in the Madame Tussaud fire.

Following the Irishman's forced removal from St Helena, Napoléon was temporarily left without a personal physician. He rejected Sir Hudson Lowe's offer of Dr James Verling, who had been the surgeon on HMS *Northumberland*, knowing full well that the new doctor's principal role would be to act as the Governor's spy. Instead, when Napoléon was taken ill in January 1819, General Bertrand selected Dr John Stokoe. He was the surgeon on HMS *Conqueror*, the flag ship of the naval force stationed at St Helena. He was also known to be a friend of O'Meara, and shared his views of the imperial exile's treatment.

As Stokoe recorded in his diary, *With Napoléon at St Helena: Being the Memoirs of Dr John Stokoe, Naval Surgeon*, published in 1901:

'The earliest idea I had of Napoléon was that of a huge ogre or giant, with one large flaming red eye in the middle of his forehead, and long teeth protruding from his mouth, with which he tore to pieces and devoured naughty little girls. I followed the Count [de Montholon] who, on coming near, took off his hat, and presented me. I did the same and made my best bow, remaining, as the Count did, with my hat off, when Napoléon, after slightly touching his, addressed me in the following words: 'Surgeon Conqueror, man-of-war. Fine ship' ... During the short time I was in the presence of Napoléon, my opinion of his character underwent a complete change. I had not been two minutes in conversation with him [in Italian] before I felt myself as much at my ease as if talking to an equal. I am not ashamed to confess that this sudden change was accompanied with such a friendly feeling towards him.'

Over a period of the next five days, Stokoe saw Napoléon four times, and immediately fell foul of Sir Hudson Lowe for:

'…discussing non-medical matters with the occupants of Longwood House, using the term patient rather than General Bonaparte in a bulletin on Napoléon's health, communicating in writing with the occupants of Longwood by giving them the said bulletin, suggesting that Napoléon was suffering from chronic hepatitis, and commenting that although there was no immediate danger, it must be presumed that in a climate where the above disease is so prevalent it will eventually shorten his life.'

Vice Admiral Plimkin

Worse still, in one report he wrote, 'the more alarming symptom is that which was experienced on the night of the 16th, a recurrence of which may soon prove fatal, particularly if medical assistance is not at hand'.

The upshot was that Stokoe was told by Vice Admiral Robert Plimkin, commander of the Royal Navy's Squadron stationed at St Helena and like Sir Hudson Lowe a rabid anti-Napoléonist), that he would be court martialled. Stokoe immediately applied for sick leave in England and returned there to plead his case with the Admiralty. Under the mistaken belief that he had succeeded, he travelled back to the island arriving there in August 1819. He was immediately arrested and tried on ten charges of illegally giving Napoléon 'favoured treatment'. With no defence counsel, and forbidden from calling any witnesses in his defence, the result of this kangaroo court was a foregone conclusion: Stokoe was dismissed the service, albeit that he was allowed to keep his pension of £100 a year. Dying in 1852 aged seventy-seven, he never managed to clear his name, but he did enjoy limited financial support from the exiled Bonaparte family. It was Stokoe's dismissal that led to Madame Mère arranging for Dr Antommarchi to travel to St Helena.

Lieutenant (later Lieutenant Colonel) Basil Jackson of the Royal Waggon Train, the forerunner of the Royal Logistic Corps, was a Waterloo veteran who served on St Helena from Napoléon's arrival until the exile's death. A fluent French speaker, with Sir Hudson Lowe's consent he shared a room with General Gourgaud at Bayle Cottage near the Governor's residence, Plantation House. This led to a good relationship with Gourgaud, who introduced him, again with Hudson Lowe's consent, to Napoléon. The Governor's plan in all of this was that Jackson would be able to report from the inside on the ex-Emperor's Household. However, it was not long before Jackson fell under Napoléon's spell and into the bed of Albine-Hélène de Montholon. He included anecdotes of his meetings with the imperial exile in *Notes and Reminiscences of a Staff Officer: Chiefly Relating to the Waterloo Campaign and to St Helena Matters during the*

Lieutenant Jackson in later life
(1794–1889)

Briars, St Helena

Captivity of Napoléon, which was published in 1877, twelve years before his death in 1889.

The most intimate account of the events on St Helena is that of Betsy Balcombe, the recipient of a lock of the imperial hair and plenty of the exile's confidences. At the start of her relationship with Napoléon she was only thirteen years old, one of four children of the East India Company's agent on St Helena. Betsy came into the imperial orbit very early on when the imperial exile was lodging in her parent's house, Briars, for three months in 1815 while Longwood was made ready for his occupation.

Nervous of meeting him, Betsy and Napoléon, who liked children, quickly struck up a friendship in which she wrapped him around her little finger. As a result, she was allowed amongst many other instances of *lèse majesté*, which included waving a sword in his face, to address him as 'Boney'. This informality aroused jealousy amongst the Household-in-Exile, who were forbidden that degree of familiarity, and suspicion on the part of the ever-suspicious Sir Hudson Lowe. As with O'Meara and Las Cases, the paranoid Governor convinced himself, on no substantive evidence, that the non-military Balcombes were helping Napoléon to smuggle uncensored letters off the island to Bonapartists in France. This led to Hudson Lowe engineering William Balcombe's dismissal from his post on a dubious charge of embezzlement, following which the family return to England in March 1818. Before this was to happen, Betsy herself became the victim of salacious British media speculation as to the nature of her entirely innocent relationship with Napoléon.

Three years after her return to England, and coincidentally in the same month as Napoléon died, the headstrong Betsy got married in haste to Edward Abell. The marriage produced a daughter but, thereafter, was short lived, with Betsy making two extended and unaccompanied visits to Australia. Eventually, she returned to England, where she wrote her account of her time in Napoléon's company, entitled: *Recollections of the Emperor Napoléon, during the First Three Years of His Captivity on the Island of St Helena: including the time of his residence at her father's house, 'The Briars'.* This intimate insight was published in 1844 and has provided historians with much material, some of which was undoubtedly inspired by the imperial exile himself, and all of which saw the events on St Helena through an imperially tinted optic. This is particularly true of Napoléon's running feud with Sir Hudson Lowe, a subject on which Betsy had no doubts as to who was in the right – and it certainly was not the Governor. However, as with Las Cases's memoirs, in the twentieth century and later the veracity of some of the material in Betsy's book has been questioned, with at least part of it being ascribed to her overly-romantic imagination.

William Balcombe (1777–1829)

From Napoléon's point of view, such later doubts would be irrelevant in his bigger scheme of things, which was to ensure that history based its judgment on *his* and no one else's *Weltanschauung*. In that, he has unquestionably succeeded, not least in the comprehensive trashing of Hudson Lowe's reputation, on which the Duke of Wellington commented:

Duke of Wellington

> '...a very bad choice; he was a man wanting in education and judgment. He was a stupid man. He knew nothing of the world, and like all men who knew nothing of the world, he was suspicious and jealous.'

A judgment with which Napoléon undoubtedly would have concurred, not least because it was probably deliberately inspired by him through the writings of O'Meara, Betsy Balcombe and others.

*   *   *

The number of books published about Napoléon by his contemporaries, and by later writers, exceeds only in the number of words the posthumous treasures, trophies and trivia of his life, reign, exile and death. Two hundred years after the 5th May 1821, the Imperial Impresario continues to fascinate biographers, historians, playwrights, film and TV directors, collectors, institutions and the general public. This interest can be claimed by no other historical figure, with the possible exception of Jesus Christ. However, unlike the Master of Europe, the relics of the Redeemer of the World – from the Turin Shroud to fragments of the True Cross – owe more to Faith than to fact.

The End, 5th May 1821

ABOUT THE AUTHORS

CHRISTOPHER JOLL MA is the regimental historian of the Household Cavalry, an advisor on militaria to auctioneers Cheffins and Sworders, a lecturer for several cruise lines, and the author of a number of books of 'faction' and fact. As an historian, he is fascinated the coincidences, quirks and trivia of history. See Christopher's entry in Wikipedia or visit *www.christopherjoll.com*.

PENELOPE, VISCOUNTESS COBHAM CBE is a Trustee of the British Napoléonic Bicentenary Trust, the Shakespeare Birthplace Trust and Chairman of the Museum Prize Trust. For 8 years she was Chairman of VisitEngland, the national tourist board, and in 2020 stood down as Director General of The 5% Club. Inter alia, she has been a Director/Trustee of Historic Royal Palaces and the V&A. See Penny's entry in Wikipedia.

Both Christopher and Penny are keen collectors of Napoléonica;
each has a room at home devoted to their collections.

INDEX

NINE ELMS
BOOKS

Nine Elms is an independent specialist imprint that is dedicated to bringing you the most creative and interesting minds in contemporary writing today.

From crime fiction and history to biography, Nine Elms features a diverse list of titles, showcasing both well established and exciting new authors.

✳ ✳ ✳

NINE ELMS BOOKS
Unit 6B, Clapham North Arts Centre,
26–32 Voltaire Road, London SW4 6DH

TEL +44 (0)20 7720 6767
EMAIL info@nineelmsbooks.co.uk
WEB nineelmsbooks.co.uk

✳

SPOILS
OF WAR

by CHRISTOPHER JOLL

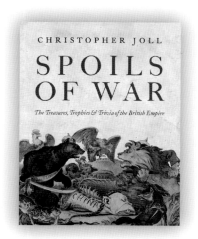

'*Each of these trophies of victory, ranging from the priceless to the valueless, has a story which Joll recounts – and sometimes debunks – with style, humour and insight*'

Michael Portillo

Over the last seven hundred years the United Kingdom has acquired a staggering array of treasures as a direct result of its military activities – from Joan of Arc's ring to the Rock of Gibraltar to Hitler's desk. *Spoils of War* describes these spoils and how they came to be acquired as well as telling the tales of some of the extraordinary (and extraordinarily incompetent) men and women, now mostly forgotten, who had a hand in the rise and fall of the British Empire. Along the way the book debunks a significant number of myths, exposes a major fraud perpetrated on a leading London museum, reveals previously unknown spoils of war and casts light on some very dark corners of Britain's military history

'*Christopher Joll has a magpie's eye for a story, combined with the dogged research skills to sniff out and solve mysteries. No one is better equipped to ignite history in this tangible and novel way.*'

Philip Mould, presenter, *Antiques Roadshow* and *Fake or Fortune?*

Hardback | 246 × 189 mm | 320 pages | Illustrated throughout | ISBN 978-1-910533-46-8   £25.00

The
DRUM HORSE
in the FOUNTAIN
& Other Tales of Heroes and Rogues in the Guards

CHRISTOPHER JOLL & ANTHONY WELDON

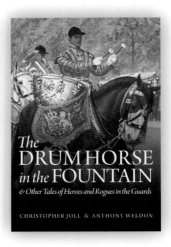

'To dip in
and out of
this book
is immensely
enjoyable.'
The Daily Telegraph

Co-authors Christopher Joll and Anthony Weldon capture the careers, accomplishments, follies and the occasional crimes of over three hundred of the officers and men, many of whom have been forgotten or overlooked, who, since King Charles II, have served in the seven Regiments of the Guards.

They have earned forty-four Victoria Crosses, founded the SAS, led the WW2 development of the Commandos and acted as spies, double agents and spy masters. Also included are extraordinary cast of characters such as the preferred candidate for the throne of Albani, one UK and two N Ireland Prime Ministers, plus a whole host of Cabinet Ministers, and an Archbishop of Canterbury, known as 'Killer', with an MC.

In other spheres, there have been championship boxers, footballers and Olympic medallists; best-selling authors, playwrights and composers; singing sensations, international musicians in the fields of pop, jazz, light and classical music as well as comedians, artists, and two Oscar-winning film stars.

Hbk | 234 × 156 mm | 314 pages | ISBN 978-1-910533-40-6 £20.00   Ebk | ISBN 978-1-910533-41-3 £4.99